The Thru-Hikers Secret

Wisdom from a Two-Time,
Joyful Appalachian Trail Thru-Hiker *by*
M.E. "Postcard" Hughes

The Thru-Hikers Secret

Wisdom from a Two-Time, Joyful Appalachian Trail Thru-Hiker

M.E. "Postcard" Hughes

Print ISBN: 978-1-48357-763-0
eBook ISBN: 978-1-48357-764-7

The first white blaze.

The Thru-Hikers Secret is a compilation of knowledge with a singular goal: to help you achieve a joyful thru-hike of the Appalachian Trail.

My past career in advertising and having a knack for simplifying the complicated provided me with a unique perspective to turn the enormity of an AT hike and its planning into simple strategies: Secrets. Hikers will be armed not just with information, but a go-to resource of answers before most will even know the questions. As the Secrets are revealed, hikers will learn what will happen and how to manage the vast texture that is an AT thru-hike.

This journey of discovery starts on the first page, continues 'til tread touches trail and travels with you to the ending terminus. From the first hour, first day, week and month, you'll move forward with greater confidence knowing you have a proven mentor. Where hiking two days may result in adversity, a thru-hike absolutely, positively will deliver it at a level of ten. Wonderfully though, decisions before and during your hike found in these pages may help to avoid "come off the trail" moments while helping you find more smiles in your miles.

The Thru-hikers Secret grew out of my first thru-hiking book *We're Off To See The Wilderness, The Wonderful Wilderness of Awes.* In it, joining my personal day-to-day account of life on the trail was a how-to section named "Have more smiles in *your* miles". Many had told me they'd read this time and again before they'd head out on an adventure. After my second thru-hike, my knowledge grew and so another, more comprehensive book idea emerged, one dedicated solely to AT preparation – *The Thru-Hikers Secret*. Since writing a book can be a time-consuming endeavor along with life's interruptions, delays happened.

When I joined REI and became an Outdoor School Instructor, I created and began teaching an AT thru-hiking in-store class under this book's name around the Philadelphia market (just 2-3 hours from the AT). Where we once averaged 5 to 8 attendees for other classes, our class attendance immediately surged to 50 participants per class. Now years into teaching it, The Thru-Hikers Secret has become a tradition in our market every new thru-hiker season.

Since I'm Postcard, you'll find many illustrations and pictures created during my actual hikes woven throughout - most by headlamp. Now, take the proverbial first step to transitioning from thru-hiking to achieving the moniker of Thru-hiker and turn the page. Enjoy the read.

Your Trail Guide

A special thank you to my fellow outdoor enthusiast and grammar guru, Dan Duffy.

He guided me through the befuddling labyrinth of semicolons, hyphens and my Yoda-esque tendencies - all which can be as treacherous as roots, rocks, and ruts.

The Big Picture.

The first step one takes in a thru-hike is the decision to go.

An Appalachian Trail thru-hike is one of the greatest gifts to yourself. It is a true-life, walking adventure in a digital, stay- put world. The journey can provide new perspectives, renewal for life and even reorder one's priorities. A thru-hike is to live large, to live simply and step beyond the timid existence of suburbia. Backpacking for months from Georgia to Maine, however, can be far from a smooth journey.

To understand all that a thru-hike entails before it is hiked is practically impossible, and yet many hikers set out on this grand adventure without a lick of experience. Imagine trying to climb Mt. Everest without ever climbing any kind of mountain? But one of the greatest aspects of the AT is that anyone can attempt it. Packs and pumps and all kinds of trail doodads are hoisted on broad shoulders, chins are raised with courage, hikers point themselves toward the horizon and take a step and then, well... everyone gets a simple lesson in gravity.

Of the couple of thousand who begin their journey on the AT each season, only a few hundred will find the rhythm of trail life and complete the 2000 miles of mountain forests. To put it simply: not making it is normal. The greater their transition from "cityness" to the hiking wilderness, the better the odds of succeeding favor them.

To no fault of their own, many will face physical and emotional adversaries they couldn't possibly have foreseen. A surprising amount of insecurities that have lay dormant - hidden deep inside them by suburban distraction - will bubble up; the isolation of the woods is a powerful trigger. Working 9 to 5 does little to prepare individuals for the enormity of a thru-hike; fortunately it doesn't limit the imagination to what may lie over the horizon.

In backpacking, going out for a couple nights, a couple weeks or a couple months are remarkably similar. The same gear is required regardless of the duration of the hike. Where they differ is in how much food you'll carry and what will find you. Challenges or adversity in a multi-day backpacking trip may indeed make their presence known, but in long-distance backpacking or thru-hiking, everything that can happen absolutely, positively will. The tangible events – rain, cold, heat, elevation gains, insects, sunshine, cool breezes, fresh air and mileage will be joined in lock step with the intangible ones - joy, elation, melancholy and despair. It is these intangible, emotional dynamics that tend to unravel many hikers' resolve of becoming a Thru-Hiker.

It's often said that an AT thru-hike is 90% mental. I'd like you to rethink that word "mental" and replace it with "emotional strength." Your emotional strength and the decisions made before and during the journey will be crucial. Safe guarding, even enhancing your emotional strength will be multi-dimensional and a top priority.

When one takes a quick glance at all that hikers face and have to adapt to, first and foremost are quite a few mountains. It is a mountain footpath after all. Where there's a footpath there's a foot and where there's a foot there's a possible blister. Traveling by foot means walking in to wildlife encounters – black bears and bull moose will flush out a cold sweat and the quick scurries of chipmunks will quicken our pulse. There'll be cold days, hot days, wet days and buggy days. Darkness will bring strange sounds and walking alone will bring up feelings of true isolation. There'll be small panic moments that you're lost, that a White blaze hasn't been seen for a while just as one comes in view…"Phew."

While there will be feelings of lonliness on the trail, one is never alone for long on the AT. Creepy crawlers and a world of dirt will be everywhere. You'll get hungry even though you'll eat all you'll see. For months you'll be carless, toilet-less and TV-less. Tripping, falling and more than your fair share of body odor will invade your clothing refusing to leave. Of all the things that will greet a thru-hiker, there is one aspect that offers the biggest challenge: managing the shear enormity.

Doing some rough math of publically-accessible numbers of thru-hike starts and completions by the Appalachian Trail Conservancy, the governing body of the AT, one discovers that of all who have set out to become a Thru-Hiker over the last decade, only 27% actually made it. A decade earlier saw an even lower completion percentage of 10%. The lightweight gear revolution over the past decade has been a contributor to the improved completion percentage. But 27% percent is still a sobering fact for many.

Having a nice, lightweight tent or hammock, a comfortable backpack and featherweight sleeping bag are all helpful for an end-to-end passage. But the most important thing to carry that increases the odds of succeeding is emotional strength.

Emotional Strength.

Many areas will determine achieving and maintaining your emotional strength:

- *The food you eat*
- *The weight your body must carry*
- *How you process adversity*
- *How you process the distance and time*
- *Finding a daily choreography that suits you*
- *Your clothing protection*
- *Transitioning from cityness to wildness*
- *When to know your hike may be in jeopardy*
- *The weight and livability of your gear*

These are the secrets that this book is all about - the secrets that will increase your odds of earning that coveted moniker "Thru-Hiker." Whether achieving that 2000-Miler status by a thru-hike attempt or section hiking if the time commitment of a thru-hike is not in the cards, all will still be relevant.

Having a previous career in consumer communications, working in an advertising agency for 25 years allowed me to hone the art of simplifying the complicated. Throughout *The Thru-Hikers Secret*, these universal truths and strategies will provide you with a pathway to keep that smile broad and ensure the journey is joyful. I can't walk your miles for you, but my secrets on how to process all that you will face will be with you every hour, day, week and month.

Earlier this year, a hiker who had attended my thru-hiking class held at REI saw me in the store and yelled, "Postcard!" Having not seen me for a year since the class, he told me he succeeded and shook my hand eleven times in three minutes. Countless others have sent me postcards from Millinocket, the exit town after reaching Mt. Katahdin, saying they carried these principals with every step they took. Truth be told, the reason I came to join REI was to help others succeed at their thru-hikes. Helping others is contagious and a selfish blessing; although the recipient of a kind gesture receives a nice boost of serotonin, so does the giver.

The secrets are proven, not all are my creation, but more the distillation of taking the complicated realities and simplifying them to understandable principals. *The Thru-Hikers Secret* is all about you having more smiles in your miles.

Questions from suburban skeptics.

A common question from those in suburbia is, "Why would anyone in their right mind want to expose themselves to the adversity and inconvenience that is a thru-hike?" Answers like, "To find adventure," or, "Live large, step outside the box," are certainly valid. Maybe it's to answer the call of the wild or to calm a stirring deep inside them? These answers are of course logical and appropriate to help others understand.

Recently though, I answered that question differently. Although I've been blessed with many talents, a singing voice is not one of them. Like most of us, I rarely do what I do poorly, so singing is never an activity I endure even when alone. Yet while on my two thru-hikes of the AT I'd find myself singing aloud, joyfully and spontaneously to the forests and mountains as I made my miles. For me, hiking the mountain forests, achieving an unsurpassed level of freedom and adventure led to such a pure elation that song, albeit off key, flowed daily in my miles.

One particular day, a hiker on the northern border of The White Mountains of New Hampshire was unfortunate enough to suddenly find herself exposed to a chorus of "Do-Re-Mi-Fa-So-La-Ti-Do" from *The Sound Of Music* before I saw her. I apologized for endangering the well-being of her eardrums. She smiled and understood how the colossal sense of freedom one can find in hiking the mountain forests can trigger childlike glee.

"What the heck is a thru-hike?" would be the other basic question to ask.

Since this book is written for those who want to attempt a thru-hike and earn the coveted moniker of "Thru-hiker", I'll briefly answer that for those who may still be in the dark. A thru-hike is a term that describes a very long backpacking trip. It means to hike from one end of a trail all the way through to the other end in a continuous journey. In the case of the Appalachian Trail on the eastern corridor of the US, it means starting at either the southern terminus on Springer Mountain in northern Georgia, or the northern terminus on Mt. Katahdin at Baxter State Park in northern Maine. Once they choose their starting point, hikers point themselves either north or south, take a step towards the horizon and start a journey that will last five to seven months on average. After about a week in the wilderness carrying everything they need to have shelter, food, safe water and warmth, they'll reach a mountain road leading to some of America's small towns and stick their thumbs out. Hitchhiking along the Appalachian Trail is not like hitching in suburbia. These locals know what these hikers are doing and know they bring commerce to their small hamlets.

Once in town, hikers will grab a room at a motel or a bunk at a hiker hostel. They'll do their laundry, shower the trail off them, resupply their food at a local grocer or pick up maildrops of food they had sent by friends or family to general delivery at the local Post Office, and then eat themselves silly at the local restaurants before heading back out. Although a thru-hike is 99% mountain forests, fresh breezes, birdsong and countless wildlife sightings, these visits to small town America are part of the texture of the thru-hike. Captured so brilliantly in the paintings of Norman Rockwell, thru-hiking the Appalachian Trail allows the hikers to not just stand outside the content of his wonderful paintings, but allows them to step inside the canvas and live among the brushstrokes.

Not the only thru-hike.

There are two other great long-distance trails in the U.S. known for thru-hikes. The Pacific Crest Trail (PCT) runs from the border of California and Mexico to the border of Washington State and Canada. Splitting the middle of the country is The Continental Divide Trail (CDT), which runs from the border of New Mexico and Mexico along the spine of the Rockies up to the border of Montana and Canada.

Each of the three great trails offer their travelers adventure and adversity in different ways. Although the PCT is the longest in terms of miles, its makeup of gentle switchback ramps that were established to help the pack mules climb with their heavy loads results in longer daily miles for most hikers. While The Appalachian Trail is the shortest at roughly 2185+ miles, it is the most taxing due to having the most vertical ascent per mile. When calculated from Georgia to Maine, the AT requires its hikers to contend with over 470,000 feet of accumulated ascent. Said differently, hikers who set out will need to climb the equivalent of Mt. Everest sixteen and half times in that single season. Some of those miles resemble nothing like most hikers' visions of a flat, hardened dirt storybook footpath. The AT requires grabbing roots and rocks to move up and forward, and boulder fields where how to make forward progress is anyone's guess.

Most hikers start their AT thru-hikes at the southern terminus in Georgia during the months of March and April. A handful begin as early as February and some as late as May. About 95% of AT thru-hike attempts are indeed northbound (these hikers are known as "Northbounders"). This approach allows hikers to start earlier in the New Year and walk with Spring. If a southbound direction is desired, hikers (known as "Southbounders") must wait until the middle of May, when Maine's Baxter State Park opens to the public. Its higher latitude often sees winter linger, forcing the Forest Rangers to be strict with start dates. If trespassers try to start before the gates open and have to be rescued from Mt. Katahdin, they can also be presented with a hefty $15,000 helicopter bill.

Still other hikers will start somewhere in the middle of the AT early in the season and plan a "flip-flop" to help avoid the hiker herds that result from the numerous Northbounders. To flip-flop is to start anywhere on the trail and head south or north. Once at a terminus or other landmark, you flip direction and complete the remaining portion – there is no one way to flip-flop. A typical flip-flop is if Northbounders are falling behind in their ability to reach Mt. Katahdin before it closes in mid-October, they can jump north and begin hiking southbound. Of course, the herds do reduce quickly as hikers discover that the AT is either physically harder or more emotionally trying (or both) than they anticipated. Whichever direction one decides to go, attrition will be high in the first weeks and months.

As in any endeavor, there is no one right way to do it. There are universal truths; things that are relevant to the many. Much will have to go right for you to pose for your completion photo, but these secrets will guard your emotional strength against the varied texture that is trail life.

Attitude and latitude.

On your mark, get set...live.

Historically, March is when the march to Maine moves into high gear. Driven either by cabin fever from winter, cityness impatience, or just plain adventurous exuberance, the masses start by the dozens every day over the next two months. This two month concentration of thru-hike starts is due mostly to the yearly closure window of the northern terminus of Mt. Katahdin on or around October 15th. If hikers fall behind schedule, making it impossible to reach Mt. Katahdin before the closing of Baxter State Park, they can always jump up north and flip-flop to continue their journey now in a southbound direction. Having completed both my thru-hikes in a continuous northbound direction, it is in this hiker's opinion that Mt. Katahdin is the finish line most worthy of the AT thru-hike achievement.

Even though the Appalachians are not giants of elevation like their cousins The Rockies or Sierra Nevada, they do put on a good show of beauty and weather adversity. A March start usually raises the odds of snow on your trek and with it a difficult passage in the higher elevations of the Great Smoky Mountains National Park. Since the eastern corridor of the U.S. is infamously wet, that precipitation means regular bouts of spring snow at elevation that will attack the resolve of every hiker. Even the most stout of them will face foes that few will have experience with. Weather just happens – snow today, storms tomorrow, and a hiker whose job it is to make miles has to push on regardless.

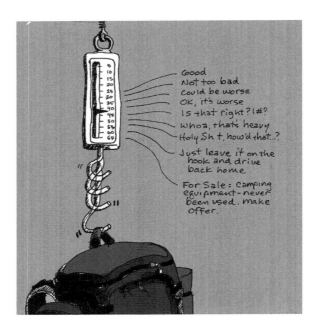

Some will go to the Amicalola Falls State Park Visitors Center - home of The Approach Trail – and hang their packs on a rusty, vintage scale at the building's corner, which I have named The Scale of Truth. It is there that hikers get a tonnage measure. Just a decade or two ago this reality check saw 50-pound backpacks as a common weight, those poor souls. These days some packs will be heavier, but thankfully, due to a revolution in light-weight gear, most will be lighter. Once some of the win-ter-weight sleeping bags and extra clothing get mailed out with the warming temps, nearly two to four pounds of pack weight will be shed. To don short sleeves and sun screen – happy happy joy joy! As the miles pass beneath their feet, more items will be removed, lightening their pack loads even more. They'll teach themselves (and hopefully abide by) AT truisms like, "If you don't use it everyday, maybe you shouldn't be carrying it."

Whether coming up the Approach Trail on foot or the forest service road by car, getting to that famous patina copper plaque that signifies the southern terminus and the AT's first 2 x 6 inch white rectangle (called a White Blaze – you'll become extremely familiar with these) is sure to be a moment of contradictions. What lies ahead is a true-life adventure, but adventure means facing the unknown – a trigger for anxiety. Some will stand there giddy, others filled with apprehension, still more feeling both. The next two months will witness an untold amount of dreamers. Yearly starting totals fluctuate, but 1800 to 3000 hikers will aim their shoes northward. At the first resupply point just 30 miles up the trail, roughly 30% will "come off the trail" and head home.

A footpath for those who seek fellowship with the wilderness.

Those who had fretted about being alone quickly learn that this will be nearly impossible – they may be hiking solo, but no hiker is truly alone. From Springer Mountain through Virginia (450 miles away), many will move in loosely banded tribes. The farther north they make it, the looser the community becomes, a network of hikers expanding north but remaining connected by chance meetings and shelter registers. Old tribes will reform into new ones, old faces from finished states will reappear out of the forests in ones still being walked – the trail is magical that way. As the miles completed increases, the number of hikers out there decreases.

The people one meets during a long distance hike is one of the most cherished aspects of the hike itself. How many ways are there to giggle? Count how many faces there are around the campfire and you'll have your answer. They'll meet tall hikers, short hikers, fast hikers and slow hikers. Thin hikers and heavy hikers are always out too, only the heavy ones are always early on and the thin ones are always later on. Some are students full of lightning and spirit while many are seniors full of patience and wisdom.

There are men chasing women, women chasing men and men and women chasing all-you-can-eat buffets. On the trail, a vegan has been known to share the same booth with a burger eater. Some hikers have retired and some are between jobs. Many knew their mission in life while others are trying to find a life with a mission. Here on the trail the wealthy and the budget minded will gel.

The young and old will bridge the gap of generations. They'll come from every state in our union – the plains and farmlands to the modern metropolitan areas. On the Appalachian Trail I've met Aussies, Brits, Irishmen, Scots, Germans, French, Canadians, French Canadians, Japanese and even Tennesseans. Their dialects will add color to the campfire talk. Out on the trail people say "Hi" and chat. Some become friends; others become lovers, husbands and wives. We're really more alike than we are different and the elements help to remind us of that. When a lightning bolt cracks near us, we all flinch in unison. All have come here for different reasons, but most are here to do as the Springer Mountain plaque states: "A footpath for those who seek fellowship with the wilderness."

What a great time, what a great feeling to cinch the pack tight to your spine and know that life will be simple for the next many months. No multitasking, no 24-hour news cycle and no putting yourself second. The next several months will be all about your own grand gift to yourself. Deciding that life, more grandly lived, can no longer be postponed. For the next 2,185- plus miles there will be no meek existence in suburbia. You're about to live large.

A new perspective.

If you've never answered the call to take a long walk along the mountains and forests of America, or if you've done so but didn't experience the ebb of your "city-ness," then its probably safe to say you think anyone who would thru-hike has to be either nuts, a misfit or a nutty misfit?

It's OK to go for a walk, even a long one.

Anyone interested in drawing becomes familiar with the dynamics of perspective. It's the visual phenomenon where 3-dimensional objects appear to recede to a location somewhere on the horizon. There is one-point perspective (the simplest), two-point perspective (the most common), and three-point which requires another axis, a vertical one. Not surprisingly, the box is an ideal shape for demonstrating all of them.

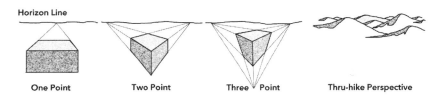

| Horizon Line | | | |
| One Point | Two Point | Three Point | Thru-hike Perspective |

However, the most dynamic perspective of all is the one gained by a thru-hike. How appropriate that it can't be shown using a box! The thru-hike perspective is about everything other than the box we tend to live and work in.

Life outside the box is a life that's difficult to discover. It's the extraordinary few that have already come to know this before that first attempt at a thru-hike. But it's the ordinary many who discover this on their hikes, and it is there it gets spliced into their DNA.

In my 2006 AT journal, I posed the question, "Does the trail change us or does the change take place first and thus results in the thru-hike?" It's the age-old quandary of the spruce grouse or the egg. When the topic is about the multiple thru-hiker, both are definitely true. Clearly not everyone finds the joy in the journey, otherwise nearly everyone would finish (short of injury or matters at home).

Which came first, the spruce grouse or the egg?

One year I met a fellow who was having the most miserable time on the hike, but his ego refused to let him stop. He truly thought anyone who would do more than one of these awful endeavors was an idiot. May I say what an absolute joy he was to be around with all his whining...his trailname should have been "Eeyore" – the doom and gloom ass from *Winnie The Pooh*.

Blessedly, many I've hiked with have discovered the magic of life on the trail. For these first-timers, they cherish the life rhythm that walking and sleeping and eating and gawking at beauty 24/7 affords. Cityness impatience is relaxed and our wilderness spirit is embraced. Each of us finds a quality that stirs, one that either awakens or reveals new takes on priorities. Don't think that we're (I should probably just speak for myself here), that I'm incomplete in some part of my life and am seeking out distraction. Maybe we all are looking for something on our first thru-hike, but to do a second or third, it's more about reuniting with aspects that were discovered.

One of the greatest blessings of a thru-hike is its simplicity. Simplicity in many forms doesn't appear instantly on a hike; it's more of a slow and seductive reveal. The farther you hike, the more multi-tasking, controlling cityness is shed. You won't always be aware of it, but eventually all the muck and melodrama of life is exorcised, leaving you engulfed in one of life's truly great pleasures: a guilt-free, stress-free, uncomplicated, one-thing-at-a-time simplicity. It's a quality that over-laps Buddhism, but you get to keep your hair and be promiscuous. I had never realized how much energy it took to orchestrate the normal complicated life until the day after my first summit of Mt. Katahdin. It was the day after this first four and a half month adventure ended - and with it my trail life simplicity that bought me to tears.

Some of us who complete a grand journey are elated with its completion for sure, but a few of us don't really need it to be over. Sure it's great to cross a finish line, but when crossing it means returning to multi-tasking every tic of the second hand, the price of a little dirt under the fingernails is a fair trade. Being a purpose-driven, goal-oriented, ladder-climbing, money-making, company-building, type-A, suit-wearing, big- title, big-car, big-home, big-overhead, cosmopolitan- professional-in-one-of-the-most-competitive-markets-in-the-world kind of guy for over 25 years, it's safe to say my foray into thru-hiking was a bit of a departure. The contradiction of it all is that trail simplicity on an AT thru-hike requires you to still be purposeful. You'll work harder physically than at any other time in your life, but I believe the body responds well to this, even flourishes in the exertion. There's nothing like purging a thousand gallons of water and sweat over five months to dissolve the sloth and mental baggage one might be holding on to.

Forever present on your hike is the grandeur of our land. Not even HD on a big honkin' flat screen can come close to it. There is nothing, I mean *nothing* like standing at the vista of incomprehensible, breathtaking beauty that spreads out infinitely to deeply touch you. You'll be converted to a new perspective on life. It's a perspective that brings a new order to our priorities. (Some experience this after having a brush with death.) A long-distance hike would be more aptly described as having a brush with life. For me it was a shift of appreciation, things to cherish more than a nice car (although I still like nice cars). Although I have never needed to be at "the" restaurant or club to see-and-be-seen, never needed the best table or the limelight (although I've had them), I now have an absolute distain for this mindset. Gossip, drama queens and kings, hissy fits and anxious ranting are seen for what they are: self-absorbed helplessness.

Clearly these are people who have lost their perspective if they ever had it. The point here is that some do multiple thru-hikes because the first provided a glimpse at a more balanced, joyful life. And I don't think I'm alone on this. As a glass half-full, optimistic soul, who laughed loud and often and joyfully chooses to walk on the sunny side of the street, it still seemed impossible to smile for five continuous months until my thru-hike.

This doesn't mean that I'm no longer materialistic; I love owning a down jacket that weighs a scant ten ounces. This doesn't mean that I've gotten lazy; walking more miles in a day with a pack than others do in a year makes you many things, lazy is not one of them. The only big negative I've seen is when some thru-hikers take on an arrogance of entitlement – that they're better than section or day-hikers, and that the world must therefore revolve around them.

The thru-hiker's perspective means having awareness of things that used to remain hidden in plain sight, and having a greater appreciation for little things and humility in the face of the bigger ones. Knowing the difference between the significant and the insignificant does not make me better than anyone else; it makes me a better me. I believe many of you will find the same.

Secret

Transition from "Cityness" to Wildness.

Do you live in a house? How about an apartment? A condo? Do you have air conditioning? You're probably used to a central heater with a thermostat that you can dial up a degree or three. You most likely have a closet filled with sweaters and coats and drawers full of toasty socks.

Most likely, all the previous are so imbedded in the everyday that they're taken for granted. Never given a second thought. *That* is about to change radically. You see, you don't become a Thru-hiker without going through quite a bit of upheaval.

I've heard stories of people planning a thru-hike for years, starting up The Approach Trail, stopping and going home. Not because the approach is difficult - which it can be - but because they had no idea what a mountain adventure would be. Thru-hiking forced us into an environment unlike anything we may be prepared to contend with. Conceptually, chasing adventure, having a vision to live large, and taking a big juicy bite out of life doesn't mean they understand all it will mean. Day One will give them a peek. Day Two will provide an emphatic confirmation of their doubts and fears.

Transitioning from Cityness to Wildness, the first hurdle.

Orchestrating this extreme new world and maintaining an optimistic outlook will determine much of your emotional strength. Find the rhythm of this mountain footpath and miles will turn into weeks that will turn into statelines. Fail to find it and mood swings resulting from hiking's minor annoyances may sour your outlook. Melancholy can find all of us at some point; stopping it and not letting it swell into despair will keep you moving forward.

How you pack your pack, how you find your choreography for the day, how you reward yourself with food and how you select your clothes can all impact how well you manage these variables. In the best of conditions, it will take discipline. In bad weather, it will take courage and the resolve to keep moving forward.

So how does one get emotionally and logistically prepared? Does one practice adversity, like intentionally walking around in the rain? Practice being cold? Well, this *is* America, so go ahead (of course, your neighbors might start to worry about you). Truth be known, I intentionally went out in the rain for practice – even the bad-ass rain. (Oh that got some looks!) Every staircase I found before my hike found me on it. Not once did I take those long escalators at the mall. Not once.

You may be a captain of industry, power suits and power lunches daily, with vast minions willing to jump up and please your every need. The Appalachian Mountains and their weather don't care. They're very democratic and uncooperative that way. If your day is orchestrating soccer practice or nine-to-nine shifts dedicated to household happiness, the Appalachians will not yield, will not ease up, will not give you a break despite your years of selflessness.

Unknown by many who arrive at that first white blaze with loaded packs, they carry things other than sleeping bags and stoves. Baggage – or life habits hidden by suburban busyness - will come along for the adventure. Walking in quiet mountain forests for hours and hours each day allows hikers to discover what lurks within. We all have baggage; it's as common as freckles. Baggage won't determine your success, but it could work against you if you're not careful.

If your impatience in life is raging, you'll have a very hard time adjusting to the speed of foot travel. Oh, you'll make progress, but maybe how you're processing that forward motion can slow your transition to wildness mode. This is a period when most are vulnerable to coming off the trail. Racing along, being driven by mileage tallies will seldom work in your favor. Making miles may be your job when attempting a thru-hike, but it is not the purpose; discovery, adventure, freedom, simplicity and joy are why many fall in love with the AT.

Have you ever affected the path of a thunderstorm? No? Good, you won't out there either. There should be no issue knowing that you will be faced with days of rain. Fortunately, some of it will be at 2am while you're already cozy in your tent or shelter – nothing like falling asleep to the sound of rain for me. With willpower or damn stubbornness, you'll hike on and sunshine will emerge and emotional power will gush. Vitamin-D induced rays will stream through the forest canopy and heat up pockets of the land. Cheeks will flush, shoulders will square and your vigor will elevate. Sunshine can be a powerful stimulant.

So when waking in the morning to the sounds of rain hitting the shelter roof or rainfly, where sinking deeper into one's mummy bag is easier than dealing with the inconvenience of rain soaked landscape, you must still motivate. Often the sounds are not rain, but the residue of treedrops falling from the wind blown canopy. Treedrops (my word) are all the raindrops clinging to the forest canopy from a nighttime shower, and a stirring breeze is sending them down to hoodwink you. The rain is over, the wetness is not, and the day and your attitude will move north. Rainbows on the horizon will beckon and laces will itch to be cinched and double knotted. (Don't want any tripping - the AT doesn't need any help at taking you down). One of the hardest moments for me is the second rainy day when I'm forced to slip on all my still-wet clothing from the day before. Wet pants, shirt, socks and shoes. It's miserable and hard to do, but it must be done. Your second outfit (the one you're wearing only in camp and for sleeping – more on this later) must stay dry and give you something to change into at the end of the second wet day, or third or fourth.

It won't be all adversity. There is grandeur and majesty and moments of perfection where the temperature and breeze and smells and birdsong will align with your adventurous spirit to outnumber the trying times a thousand-fold. The good, the splendidly joyful, "glad to be alive" days, do not make one end his or her hike.

In the aftermath of a rainstorm, you'll wake to a wonderful morning. The mountain air will be washed and rinsed of all foreign bodies. Without all the motor traffic to replenish it, you'll be engulfed in such a purity of air that it will get inhaled deep where it will build a memory.

One of my most significant post-hike adjustments was a new craving for fresh air. Windows, albeit the house or car, were left open and now, years later, nothing has changed. Apparently, fresh air agrees with us humans. You will feast on freshness out there. In fact, just using the word fresh seems trivial to how incredible it is. Maybe a new spelling to give it more umph? Maybe "fffresh" makes it more vivid?

There'll also be a different kind of moisture that you will contend with: humidity. We probably all have experience with humidity, so it isn't as difficult of an adjustment. You'll need to drink constantly. I remember one day moving through New York, it was 90% humidity with 90 degree temps. The distance I covered that day was farther than a marathon. Six liters of water with electrolytes, six sodas from an opportunistic hot dog stand, a Bud and a bottle of Poland Spring from Trail Magic (kind gestures from others not hiking the trail in the form of coolers filled with goodies). Traversing the Mid-Atlantic States can be a very humid affair, and you will almost immediately sweat out any liquid that your drink. Staying hydrated will keep your endurance up while fending off leg cramps, a task made all the more difficult when you're sweating like a waterfall.

After days and weeks of the soupy moisture, your journal starts to get a bit more creative in describing it. In 2006, my journal featured an illustration of me climbing a mountain while a school of tuna swam by heading down-mountain.

All these tangible adversaries will become commonplace in the first months. How you react to them, how you process them, is what determines the intangible; your elevated joy or tussles with low moods.

The first hurdle to be faced in an attempted thru-hike is the transition from what I have coined one's cityness to wildness mode. Wildness is another state of mind, a more patient, flexible and balanced mindset. First used by John Muir, he suggested that wildness in ones life was a necessity. Transitioning to wildness in an AT thru-hike will absolutely be a necessity.

Not only does the trail and its texture change from state to state, but also amazingly so do you. Cityness is your current state of mind, your go-go, multitasking impatience that comes with the pressure of managing business and life in suburbia. How well you transition to the wildness of battling gravity, mountain elevation and constantly changing weather events will determine how broad your smile will be in the early stages of your thru-hike. This transition involves letting go rather than go-go, staying in the moment rather than multitasking, and relaxing your ego along with the need to control everything.

Cityness	Wildness
Go-Go mentality	Let go
Impatient	Patient
Multi-tasker	Stay in the moment
May think wants are needs	Knows they're different

Can't be inconvenienced	*Flexible*
Ego / Controller	*Land/nature are the boss*
Laughs at others	*Laughs at themselves*

(Cityness can also be those extra pounds that find some of us from our excessive sofa sitting.)

Where once you'd fret about the numerous mountain climbs to be faced that day and their toll on your body in the first weeks and months, at some point that will give way to a "doesn't matter what's in front of me, I'm going over it" attitude. Once you face and climb the AT mountains, along with the passage of time in doing so, an ever increasing empowerment and resolve will overtake you. You'll just go, leaving your frets several state-lines behind you. It's a wonderful and powerful inner spirit that you will harness. Until that takes place, everything you do and every decision you make will likely be guided by cityness.

Whether you hike The Approach Trail or not, the decision to avoid it by way of a car ride on a forest road is more of your cityness guiding you rather than your wildness mode guiding you. After all, it's nearly nine miles of up that doesn't count.

The Approach Trail archway behind the Amicolola Falls State Park Visitor Center. The laughs and misery begin.

However, it's estimated that in addition to the 2000-plus miles they're already taking on, a thru-hiker will travel an additional 250 miles walking to the shelters, water sources and privies, along with running errands around town. If getting driven by the forest road is taken, hikers must still hike backwards nearly a mile to reach the first white blaze. The decision to take The Approach Trail may be an early glimpse into one's emotional readiness to face all that the AT is. However, it does not determine either way whether hikers will achieve their goal of becoming a Thru-hiker. The Approach Trail is more of a tradition, and if it were faced in month two it wouldn't be of any consequence. Early on though, those first 8.8 miles of up that do not count towards achieving a thru-hike is all about your emotional readiness.

You don't have such a choice if a southbound thru-hike is the goal. The starting northern terminus of Baxter Peak on Mt. Katahdin in Baxter State Park, Maine, is 5.2 miles of trail much tougher than The Approach Trail. There is no forest service road choice.

Your transition will be similar to moving to a new house in a new town. Everything you knew as normal and routine has been erased. But one morning you wake up and suddenly there's a new sense of serenity, a new inner peace with your surroundings. That's when all that is new and abnormal becomes normal; that's when a house transitions into a home.

An important factor in the cityness-to-wildness transition will be your conditioning, pack weight and footwear choice. The better your aerobic climbing endurance, the less victimized you'll be. Pack weight and footwear will be addressed in a later section, but let it be known, everyone hikes with a wider smile carrying 25 pounds rather than 45.

There's an old saying that I never agreed with which is "to hike yourself into shape." It is hard to attain thru-hiker fitness without carrying a backpack up and down the Appalachians, so getting a limited-time health club membership before your tread touches trail can be helpful. This phrase also seems to echo a touch of laziness in some ways. Rather than looking for ways to limit the effort required, one's fitness level can provide even the most apprehensive beginner with confidence. Before each thru-hike I got myself a three month membership and worked on that older style Stairmaster, spending an hour at a time, increasing the level of difficulty each time and leaving drenched in an empowering sweat. Starting in Georgia and then hitting North Carolina, the ascents are constant and the attacks on your outlook are daily. Having better conditioning before you start your hike will minimize becoming a victim to all the excessive elevation gains and losses. Without some pre-hike conditioning, you'll grow to detest land features called gaps. (Heck, they'll annoy you even if you do start your thru-hike physically fit).

Gaps are those transition areas between a descent and yet another ascent. It would be lovely if after a hard ascent you never had to give that elevation back, but no, you have to hike back down to a "gap" and then face yet another up. Remember, when the journey is the equivalent of sixteen Mt. Everest's, what goes up must come back down before going back up. PUDs are another trail phrase to describe the gaps tormenting presence. PUDs stand for Pointless Ups and Downs and there is no shortage of them on the AT.

The climbs will be a constant assault on your thighs and glutes. The descents will attack the knees and the muscles surrounding them. Giving them some acclimation at a health club will reduce their trial by fire in the first weeks; plenty of hikers have stopped in the first few days and headed home who adhered to the "hike yourself in to shape" adage.

If you can't swing the health club then certainly get walking. Increase your foot travel with every errand to the mall by parking out farther from the front door. (Even famous martial arts master Bruce Lee expressed this same wisdom in his book *The Tao of Jeet Kune Do.*) This always reminds me of that puzzling question why so many try to find the closest parking spot to the front door of their health clubs? It's OK to get fitness inside, but how inconvenient to be forced to get some outside the facility by walking in from a distant parking spot! Sigh...

Getting out for more fitness walks of 3, 4, 6 or more miles at a good athletic pace will also help with your leg strength and endurance. Along with the health club visits, I bet my legs got at least 500 miles of fast-paced, long-ish duration walking before hitting the trail. This doesn't have to be done with a backpack either, just getting out frequently so your muscles are prepped for the daily attack helps. As you progress, try to push your envelope of fitness. If you aren't returning soaked in perspiration, you may not be achieving as high a level of acclimation as you could. *Only you can monitor your fitness level.*

The planned morning start of my second thru-hike up The Approach Trail ran into a snag when my Amtrak arrival at Gainesville, Georgia, was hours late. Unable to start my ascent until 1pm (!#!*?!#), thanks to my pre-hike conditioning I touched that first white blaze atop Springer Mt. at 4pm – just three hours to ascend that infamous first climb with a full pack on my back. A near 3 mph pace uphill on Day 1! Not too shabby. Skip the misguided "hiking yourself into shape" drivel.

Stay In The Moment...or else.

Sorry for the scare tactics, but there's an epidemic in the land. Almost no part of one's life has been immune to contracting it. Multi-taskingitis may help us seize the day in business and help us orchestrate home life, but multi-tasking is the enemy of the long-distance backpacker.

In a world of guardrails, traffic warning signs, anti-slip surfaces and smooth, civilized ramps, it's easy to move from point A to B without consequence. However, what if we take ourselves to an environment where guardrails are removed. Warning signs are dug up. Slippery, awkward, pitched and irregular ground becomes the norm. Multi-tasking can take you down and on the AT, out. Heck, even while paying attention the AT can still take you down...and it will. You will fall hard. You will fall soft. But you will fall less if you stay in the moment and pay attention while hiking. Frankly, you cheat yourself of experiential bliss during the journey if you're not in the moment.

Since falling is common on the AT but rare in suburbia, you may not have much practice at processing these mishaps. It would be easy to get down on yourself or get angry, or even feel you're weak. I suggest you try what

I did every time I took a tumble: "That's one" or "That's sixteen". Of course, I'm no philosopher, I could never compete with the wisdom that has been around for a thousand years in the Asian cultures. Who would have thought that these brilliant philosophers had already perfected thru-hiking principles.

"Our greatest glory is not in never falling, but in rising every time we fall."

~ Confucius

"Beginning is easy – Continuing is hard."
"Fall down seven times, get up eight."

~ Japanese Proverbs

Multi-tasking in an office or home is a bit different than doing it from behind the wheel of a car or on the trail. In a car it can lead to serious events that raise your auto insurance and your likelihood of a court date. On the trail, it can lead to injury, broken body parts, or even death. Your worst enemy is not a black bear - it's you not paying attention. Staying in the moment is a decision, a habit you'll need to embrace to increase your odds of making it. There are zero non-slip surfaces, and hand-rails are rare. There are two warning signs though; one is in The Whites informing you that people die of exposure there (it is a beautiful, treacherously difficult parcel of land). The second presents itself at the start of the 100-Mile Wilderness in Maine strongly suggesting you have ten days of provisions. My council is to embrace a new habit when you thru-hike: become a world class single-tasker and stay in the moment.

With its slower pace, footspeed may also agitate your level of impatience once trail life begins. You'll have the feeling that it's taking forever to get somewhere. Adjusting to two or three miles per hour rather than 55, 65 or whatever (80!) you drive may prove frustrating. One challenge I give all participants who attend my Thru-Hikers Secret class at REI, which helps acclimation to these slower dynamics, is to start driving the speed limit, especially the month before your start date. This simple change of habit results in good psychological patience practice that you're not falling behind when everyone else is whizzing past you. You can embellish your driving-the-speed-limit patience practice if you do so without having music on. This will heighten single-tasking in a quieter environment. Do you know what single-tasking in a quieter environment is also called? Hiking.

SPEED 55 · · · · · · · · · · · · > **SPEED 2.5**

Coming to grips with your cityness (habitual multi-tasking go-go) and dialing up your capacity of patience will have its benefits for the entire journey.

The saying "Avoid going too far too fast with too much too soon" is a slogan on the trail that tries to address that cityness impatience which can result in unnecessary blisters, chaffing, or possible hike ending injuries. The enormity of the journey and that go-go mindset has many believing that they have no time to pause and address that friction hot spot on their foot. So they tell themselves it will go away or that they are tough and can take it. Usually what happens next is a rather large, painful blister followed by sitting in a motel or hostel for a week. During a resupply rest stop in Hiawassee, Georgia, I met a hiker who got his trailname "Six Toes" from one of those blisters-by-denial.

Your cityness go-go will be paired with your exuberance to start your grand adventure, but beware: this combination of attitude could possibly push you into trouble. Your desire to live large will be raging. This will subside a bit as time moves forward, but it may contribute to delaying your discovery of patience. Once you find the serenity of letting go, those feelings of perpetually being behind in life will vanish and no Tibetan monk will have anything on you.

Letting go of one's go-go doesn't mean hikers aren't purposeful, though. Moving with purpose, regardless of the weather, is the only way statelines are crossed.

Maybe the most difficult dynamic of cityness to come to grips with is your ego. We all have ego, some bigger than others. A strong sense of self is a good thing. As mentioned earlier, in order to combat the countless opinions one must contend with daily in the world of business, having a healthy ego is essential. In a grand gesture of democracy, the Appalachian Mountains could care less if you are a captain of industry with millions in the bank or if you're living paycheck-to-paycheck. The mountains will treat us all as equals. I for one like that - it's not who you know, but rather if you personally have the fortitude and tenacity to accomplish the task. Nothing will be given through back office arranged agreements under the cover of night. It will have to be earned.

Yielding to the true bosses of the AT – the elevation gains, gravity, weather and difficulty, may be a bit more challenging for those who feel they have had complete control over their city and suburban kingdoms. You don't control the Appalachians; you manage your passage of them. That's not to say you can't orchestrate your thru-hike with aplomb, it's just that the mountains will force you to relearn humility. In North Carolina, I encountered a former US Senator who was having a terribly low moment. Used to privilege and power, he was mired deep in despair that he could not have influence over the mountains, weather, mileage – a humbling period in this person's life for sure. I paused my hike and spoke and listened and offered some perspective for an hour. I would later learn he continued on all the way to New Hampshire where he ran out of time in the season. The texture of a 2000 mile adventure that is voluntary can weaken the most stout, most accomplished of us. Respecting the difficulty of a thru-hike will allow your ego to take a sabbatical.

Having had a career that turned me into a million-miler with airlines and growing up as a Disney kid (about 50 + visits) means I also grew up believing in the phrase "It's a small world." You discover the opposite when you walk it. The world is quite large and foot speed pounds that in to you every step. Training in Chicago for my first thru-hike had me realize those miles on flat bike trails around Lake Michigan was a wee bit easier than miles on the Appalachian Trail. But we find our confidence, we let go and just go, and we get a handle on our ego accustomed to control, and transition to managing what we can. With newly found humility, you will keep moving forward forever hoping that your smiles outnumber your miles.

Seeing the USA the AT way.

One of the most charming aspects of an AT thru-hike is the numerous visits down Main Street America. Although the trail is 99% woods, mountains and wildlife, visits to small towns like Hot Springs, North Carolina always brings a smile to this hiker. Here the children call their parents Pa and Momma. They're more beer drinkers than wine drinkers and a visit to the Tractor Supply Store is one where everyone piles into the truck. You can walk the length of town in four minutes; there is no traffic light to slow you down. The people of these small towns embrace the commerce that comes with the hiker bubble of March into May. We help them, they help us.

The Post Office closes for lunch and the daily special down at the diner usually involves something with gravy. Woven into the texture of this town are the hikers, walking up and down doing the necessary chores, others with loaded packs stuffed to the zippers with a resupply of food headed north, following little white rectangles back out to the mountain forests of the Appalachians.

What goes on here goes on everywhere in America every day (taking us hikers out of the picture). It's the backbone of this country, the small places that Interstates detour around so those in a hurry are not bothered.

We, who are traveling by foot, adapt easily to their pace. The countless miles reintroduce us to patience, along with a down- home politeness. I feel the tug to say, "Yes Ma'am" and "'Preciate it," with a touch of country in my voice. In turn, we too are treated with warmth and a generosity that comes to them naturally. Most who hike the

Appalachian Trail haven't any idea what awaits them. Hikers who have survived the first 271 miles here to Hot Springs have a fair chance to reach Damascus, Virginia, known as the "Friendliest Town on the Appalachian Trail," and home to the yearly celebration of past and present hiker seasons, called "Trail Days". Sometimes the trail brings us to them and then sometimes it's our thumb. Bunks are obtained, rooms are reserved and chores are commenced. Our Zero's help us get stronger with rest while our Nero's keep our wallets fat and moving on. Reaching these small towns, some of which are milestones, are every bit as important as the 13 statelines.

*Hitchin' to town in the back of a pickup because you have a bit
of an aroma. Showers, laundry and all things "normal" will
be the order of the day. It matters little if it's 3 miles or 10 once
those wheels start turning. Small town USA, here I come.*

(I had never hitch-hiked until I hiked the AT)

Secret

Managing the Enormity – Think Small.

A thru-hike can be a joyful stroll through a child's vision of a storybook footpath. Meandering along mossy forests where dappled sunlight warms the trilliums and Juncos take flight to fly in front of your footsteps.

It is also a place where the smooth and whimsical are replaced by the rugged and taxing. And the rugged replaced with the "You've got to be kidding" gut busting tough. Pause for a moment and visualize the hardest rain you've ever witnessed...(Got it visualized? Good.) Now picture yourself hiking in it. This type of rain – along with the frequently accompanying thunderstorms - are common on an AT thru-hike.

While the physical demands of a thru-hike are significant, the emotional demands are just as great. However, these tangible, physical adversities are not what end the majority of attempts. That is reserved for the intangible, emotional ones – melancholy, low moments, and even despair are the unraveling for many a hiker. Thank goodness the joy found surpasses the malaise. Other than injury, most who don't make it get mired in emotional distress. Managing your emotional strength with the decisions made before and during the hike will be crucial.

If you have a pulse there may be a fret or three.

Whatever we're afraid of one year might not be the case the next. My niece was once afraid of meatloaf, go figure? Or my nephew likes to stay as far away from condiments as he can - yeah, flusters me to no end ever since I became the cook of the family gatherings. But that's OK, my Dad taught me well over the years. In fact, where cooking Thanksgiving dinner scares the stuffing out of many, I love it. Bring it on.

A thru-hike will absolutely scare the electrolytes out of some, but in totally different ways. Managing your fears will be necessary to making it to Katahdin. If you have a pulse (you are reading this) you're going to fret before and during your big hike. I certainly did.

Topping the list of common fears before and during a thru-hike are bears. The tendency is to grab on to the mauling stories rather than to realize how rare these stories are. The list of fears also includes isolation, bugs, cold, rain, cold rain, and snakes. All give many a hiker pause. All are real, but each is different from hiker to hiker. (Bear attacks may be the least likely of the lot, so relax.)

I met one hiker whose fear was walking underneath those crackling high power lines the AT occasionally passes beneath – a non-issue with me, but for her, she'd stop and wait for another hiker to appear and then get escorted. True story.

Of all the things that will greet a thru-hiker, there is one aspect that offers the biggest challenge, only most haven't any warning of it before they start. For most of us, the hardest part of an AT thru-hike will be managing the sheer enormity.

Our normal life doesn't give us much experience at dealing with this enormity. Gargantuan in scope, lengthy in distance with a timeframe measured not in hours, but four, five, six or more months of primitive living. Life on the mountain footpath involves everything tangible and intangible and often happening at the same time. It can unhinge your mental and emotional confidence. Wonderfully though, there is a strategy in dealing with that enormity, and that is to Think Small.

Think Small is a strategy that has worked for me and countless others, even if they didn't put those exact words to it. Think Small means to focus on where you want to end up at the end of the hiking day. That could be a shelter. It could be a campsite. It could be a time on the clock.

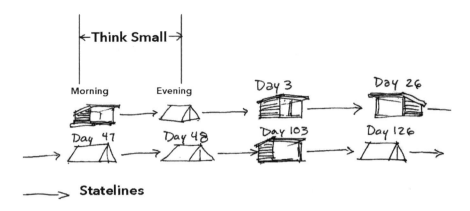

Statelines

Think Small means you hike to that night's destination.

Tomorrow, you hike to *that night's* destination.

Think Small means you let go of the enormity. Let go of fourteen states. Let go of four, five, six or seven months. Let go of 2,185-plus miles. Let go of counting down miles left or miles completed. Think small means you focus on the day only. It means you enjoy the day. Then you enjoy the next day. Make camp. Make camp again. Stay in the moment. Hike the day only. Days will inevitably become state lines.

During my first hike, this strategy appeared to me on day eight. Everyone was asleep in the shelter and I had the campfire to myself. Coyotes were battling across the valley to see who had the loudest howl. It's fair to say a touch of melancholy was in me. Although the weather had improved, I was still adjusting to the bigness of the land and the slowness of foot travel. I decided that tomorrow I would only concern myself with where I wanted to get to. That I would let go of everything and just enjoy the day and see what could be seen. If I had a good time then the next day I'd go out to have fun that day and so on and so on.

Astonishingly, I had a great next day – the best of the adventure to that point. As the week progressed, focused only on my end of the day location, I was hiking more free, smiling more. Later, when writing my first book, I put the words Think Small to this secret. Let me be candid: if I wasn't Postcard, my trailname could be Cupcake (I'm not emotionally invincible). To head into each hiking day with one destination in mind, then to reach it and feel the pride of reaching it, all while letting go of the enormity and letting go of all that lay ahead was crucial. By doing so I started to process the hike in more simplistic terms. Rather than a gargantuan expedition against-all-odds, hell-or-high-water, over a diabolical landscape of epic proportions and relentlessly tough conditions, I reduced the endeavor to its core level with an "Ah-Ha" moment:

"A thru-hike is just a whole bunch of day hikes."

Psychologically, it is much easier to manage one day rather than 180 of them. Not only have I not seen any value in thinking of the bigness of the adventure, but it can be detrimental to your emotional strength. Take a bad, cold, wet day and wed that to a mindset consumed by all that still lies ahead, all that must be overcome, months more to go, thousands of miles more. Do that and you attack your own resolve, your own emotional strength. To use a common phrase: you become your own worst enemy.

Let me explain this a way thru-hikers can understand. You can't eat a whole large pizza in one bite. By taking it in one bite at a time, one slice at a time, the whole thing will eventually be in your belly. Think Small.

What was that?

Whether you're at home or in your car, if you hear something out of the ordinary, it triggers an alarm. Now imagine going out to the mountain forests where few dare to tread. Now imagine how alarms go off with every tic or snap or whatever sound. Toss in some darkness without doors and deadbolt locks and your imagination runs to borderline panic.

In the early days of your thru-hike, when cityness and wildness haven't transposed fully, the tiniest sound can make you jump. After all, there are bears and rattlesnakes and 900-pound rutting moose in them there woods, aren't there? And today there's no shortage of news channels telling you why you should be terrified to set foot outside your door. Being a tad bit on edge, I found my forest fright from two main culprits – a panicked chipmunk, and, the one that always got my neck hairs to stand, the dreaded Rufous-sided Towhee (a bird).

Most towhees, after attending their famous Bird Academy for the Pursuit of Hiker Hysteria, land their first job along the AT. It is there they start a career of kicking up the forest undergrowth just as we scaredy-cats come along. (Yeah, sort of mean spirited on their part, don't you think?) I've lost track of how many times I was startled by a scurrying, panicked chipmunk or towhee early in my hikes until my wilderness acclimation was complete. One hiker from England who had the same overreaction to these tiny creatures earned her trailname, "Sees Bears Everywhere."

The sound that sends chills up some hikers' spines is the Ruffed Grouse. About the time we start moving north, Ruffed Grouse start their mating wing-thumping. Sounding absolutely nothing like a bird, (perhaps a Pterodactyl would be closer- since we all know what those sound like) these grouse will pound their wings like a distant beating drum. Visions of tribal warpath ceremonies may be conjured, or that of an escaped Silverback gorilla beating its chest. Amazing how what is basically a forest chicken can conjure these fears. This is the consequence of lifting our butts off the sofa and going to where the wild things are.

As our quest for adventure unfolds, the sudden rattling sound of a Timber Rattler is sure to be heard as the temps climb. Although that castanet vibration can rock the most hearty of us, it is nice to get a warning rather than just biting us as we pass. Truth be told, despite all the Hollywood movies, many bites by rattlers are dry bites. Dry bites are still very painful, only the venom isn't released since they're not hunting, just striking out of fear (even snakes are scaredy-cats). As the adventure continues you may come to celebrate all the wildlife sightings that enrich the thru-hike experience, as was the case for me. Just for fun, I'd keep a mental tally of all my animal encounters: 156 Whitetail Deer, 9 Black Bear, 5 Moose, 18 Palliated Woodpeckers, 6 Ruffed Grouse... Recognizing and celebrating the wildlife adds richness to the journey.

A sound that frightens no one, and of which my ears are especially fond of is the Black Throated Blue Warbler. Reminds me of someone's cell phone ringing – quite electronic with a touch of echo as if a hiker lost his phone in a cave while spelunking (yes, I have a vivid imagination). You just wait. I bet one of you this hiking season will hear this sound and say, "Whose phone is ringing?"

The Appalachian woods have many Barred Owls, known for their distinct hoot of "Who cooks for you? Who cooks for you- allll?" Yet it's the tiniest owl, the Eastern Screech Owl, that is the fiercest sounding – sort of like the shriek of old rusty door hinges opening in anger. Owls and the Common Loon are my favorite on a thru-hike; they speak to the wilderness and of adventure in far off places. Upon arrival in Maine, the state's countless lakes make loon encounters frequent. Since several Lean-to's sit near these ponds and lakes, the loons arrive just before sunset and start their haunting serenades, a symphony that fills me with peace. Their yodel finds us deep into our journeys, after we've strip away all the complication of the normal world and are simply moving, breathing, sleeping. We find ourselves talking less now and listening and watching more as another sunset burns the sky with gold, orange and fuchsia.

If you're using shelters on your journey, the whisper-soft pitter-patter of mice feet will unnerve you if you forget your iPod or earplugs. If you have neither when one of your fellow hikers launches into their snoring symphony, well, trust me, you should probably just go set up your tent. Hikers with trailnames like "Chainsaw" don't have them because they once were a lumberjack. It's totally unfair how the snorers are the ones that always fall asleep first; maybe cruel would be more accurate?

If you're tenting out, those earphones, earplugs, or Advil PM can also help when 400 pounds of heavy breathing really *is* on the other side of your nylon fortress (hey, if you can't hear it, maybe it's not there?). Or when the movement of leaves from a field mouse makes one think 80-foot anaconda. Nothing is beyond our imagination early in our thru-hike.

We've all probably heard that when one of our senses is reduced another is heightened. As forest silence replaces suburban cacophony, our ears and eyes start detecting slight changes a bit more easily (in my completely unscientific observations). Topography of the land will influence some of these observations - acoustic shadows or the channeling of sound between hillsides will both happen. A low decibel ruckus in the woods often says a line of rain is fast approaching; other times it's just a surprise waterfall.

After many days in the woods it won't be hard to pick out the sound of humanity, the unmistakable hum of hard rubber on pavement and V-8's whirling by. Despite our love of being out there, that hum always sits well with many of us because where there's a road there's a town and where there's a town there's a restaurant.

After a significant time in the woods, with calorie deficit grabbing you firmly by the stomach, that road holds the promise of the most cherished thing a long-distance hiker can hear. Like a Siren song, you know you'll soon be hearing, "May I take your order?"

The news reported last hiker season that an estimated 300,000 American's had died that year from sitting too much. And you thought trekking off into the mountain forests was dangerous?

Secret

Eat happy. Hike happy.

What you eat during your thru-hike can be your secret weapon.

Eat food that's beneficial and your body will be fueled to attack the day. But food as fuel requires it getting inside you. I don't know about you, but I'm unable to just shove food in my mouth that doesn't taste good. So liking your food will be pivotal on many different levels.

You've put yourself in the abnormal environment of the mountain forests, living an abnormal life of backpacking day after day, week after week. Everything you've ever known in normal life is gone. Although you may be chasing adventure and the achievement that is a thru-hike, all that change can attack your resolve and whittle away at your emotional strength. What you choose to eat can actually normalize the abnormal.

After about two weeks on the trail, there's a wonderful place on the AT called The Nantahala Outdoor Center (NOC) that sits at a picturesque location by the Nantahala River, a whitewater nirvana for kayakers. Bunk space, private rooms and larger rooms can all be had for a fee. There's an outfitter for gear adjustment and upgrades. They accept maildrops and have laundry facilities. Most important of all is the River's End Restaurant. Depending on one's pace, the River's End Restaurant offers thru-hikers a menu of culinary bliss and an ideal place for a zero day right on the trail, which I took on both my thru-hikes.

It was at this point during my first thru-hike that I found all my trail food - the food I thought I was supposed to carry - was making me feel less than joyful. Unfortunately, just because your food bag is stuffed with all the acknowledged trail foods most places sell, it doesn't mean your taste buds will be happy. A solution to my food unhappiness found me by accident.

The morning I was about to head out on that long 7 mile climb of Cheoah Bald out of the NOC, it occurred to me to order an extra breakfast sandwich "to go." Without realizing it at the time, that one breakfast sandwich I'd enjoy hours later atop Cheoah Bald revealed a food strategy: life on the trail didn't have to be all trail food. All of a sudden, the normalcy of a breakfast sandwich with its English muffin, bacon and egg taste in the wilderness, rather than simple trail mix, put pep in my step. Many start their hikes with the common trail mix (GORP – Good Ol' Raisins and Peanuts). OK, but if you don't eat GORP now, Monday through Sunday, then why choose it for what may be the hardest endeavor of your life? It can provide beneficial fuel, but once again, if it doesn't please you from a taste stand point it's only doing half the job. Taking real town food into the trail made the abnormal a touch more normal and with it I had a happier, stronger outlook.

"Normalize your food, every day doesn't have to be trail food."

On my next town visit-and-resupply, the trail mix was willingly, joyfully swapped out for a large bag of Fritos that I dumped into a gallon Ziploc. Providing salt, fat, calories and normal suburban-life good taste, Fritos offered me food I was familiar with. Energy bars - beneficial, but bad tasting to me - turned into string cheese, summer sausage and cupcakes. Each night after dinner I'd have hot chocolate and some fancy cookies or something sweet to reward my day's achievement and offer culinary comfort. Conveniently packaged individually, I liked the bigger, richer Land O'Lakes hot cocoa – ideal for backpacking. Bringing food tastes that agreed with me to the trail during this most extreme of activities did wonders for my mood.

This new strategy proved valuable every step forward. By making these small food adjustments from everything being "trail" to some foods I would associate with our normal lives in suburbia, my food happiness bloomed, and with it my emotional strength. It's appropriate here to repeat: Eat happy. Hike happy.

Since my trail food epiphany at the NOC, I continued to build on this strategy even further every time I headed back out to the woods. Whenever I left town I'd carry real town food back to the trail to enjoy that night – a foot-long from Subway or burgers or chicken nuggets for that day's lunch and dinner. When the majority of your dinners are one-pot meals of noodles or rice dishes, having a sandwich with real bread and other flavors breaks the food monotony. It compliments the Think Small strategy that each day is just a day hike. (Only one caution: avoid tomato on sandwiches because the high moisture content will turn the bread all mushy.) Additionally, I filled up my backpack reservoir with 2 liters of Gatorade Fruit Punch. It was like drinking candy until the wilderness water supplanted it. Good tasting and had some umph!

One area of food where I totally nailed it was breakfast. For both my thru-hikes I used a meal replacement powder for a high calorie, high carb, high protein milkshake. My favorite is Muscle Milk. By putting two scoops in a Ziploc and including it in my maildrops, I got a super beneficial, super fast, easy way to have some killer fuel. The 32 grams of protein, 310 calories, and 19 grams of carbohydrates all powered me forward and accelerated my leg muscle development. Never did I bonk on a hiking day after starting with this lactose-free breakfast milkshake. Vanilla Crème and Chocolate Malt made me the most giddy, but strawberry, pina colada, orange crème, blueberry and others had me looking forward to it every morning.

For me, a Muscle Milk shake is like having liquid ice cream – just add water to the powder in a Tupperware milkshaker (which I carried rather than a cup), shake, drink, rinse, pack up and go. Fast and easy cleanup allowed for quick exits from camp to start making miles. As briefly mentioned, I had energy bars that could be categorized as super fuel, only most tasted dreadful. Sort of hard for your food to do some good if you don't want to eat it. They got swapped out for Kellogg Nutri-Grain cereal bars that are all along the AT. I usually had two of the Mixed Berry along with my morning shake just as I started hiking.

The food you choose needs to meet five standards:

- *Good calories for energy*
- *Good carbohydrates for endurance*
- *Good protein for recovery*
- *Light in weight because you're a backpacker*
- *Great tasting for emotional strength*

These criteria eliminate the use of MRE's (Meals Ready-to-Eat) on thru-hiking that are standard fare for the military. MRE's by law are required to be one-and-a-half pounds per meal – thus not delivering on #4 above. In fact, three or four days of Knorr brand (found in most grocery store side-dish aisles) pasta or rice side dishes for dinner will weigh what one MRE would. We'll discuss later the weight of gear, but your food weight will be just as important to manage.

Your own dietary desires will factor in heavily as to whether or not you use maildrops. Maildrops do not limit one's freedom in a thru-hike; you'll need to go into towns regardless to resupply. Doing so with maildrops gives you a touch more control. It ensures that you're getting what makes you happy, and a visit to the local Post Office is no more limiting than a visit to the local grocery store. One important thing to understand is that an AT thru-hike is not like hiking in the Alaskan wilderness where resupply points are few and hikers need to burden themselves with ten days to two weeks worth of food. An AT thru-hike means only needing to carry four to six days of provisions at any point. However, my one rule of thumb was to carry one extra dinner for "what if's".

Thanks to all those Norman Rockwell-esque small towns, resupply is easy and often. Additionally, the AT is not about survival. It is an incredibly difficult adventure, but it is well marked and the logistics of easy resupply allow for frequent pauses from the constant assault of weather, rocks and gravity. If you want your hike to be one of foraging, then hey, knock yourself out. But that is not common for a thru-hike on the AT.

Now, there's no guarantee that the food you send to yourself will still be desired if you never vary your food. Food monotony can set in if you eat too much of the same thing, so even with doing maildrops you'll most likely still visit the grocery store to buy real town food for your zero day or the next section of your hike. I actually carried a compact wine cork opener in my food bag. On zero days I'd get a bottle of wine to enjoy. Just because you're thru-hiking doesn't mean it has to be a foray into deprivation.

Since the AT travels through the most densely populated part of America, opportunistic food will present itself regularly. Enjoying food one doesn't have to carry is, in a word, AWESOME. Throughout the journey the trail will cross roads where diners sit a few tenths of a mile to the trail's left or right. Sometimes the AT will emerge from the forest directly in front of a Dairy Queen or convenience store. Swinging into these opportunistic places to get flavors that aren't in your backpack will boost your spirit. Your taste buds will be absolutely jazzed.

In North Carolina, I stopped by a small roadside restaurant that the guidebook said was just a half-mile *up* the hill (yeah, hill). But once that hearty, heaping plate of town food gets set down in front of you after days in the woods, the half-mile-uphill-that-doesn't-count becomes a distant memory. After I ordered my four eggs, two orders of hash browns, two orders of English muffins, four orders of bacon and a large OJ and coffee, I included two double cheeseburgers to go. The waitress just said,

"Sure, Honey," since she had experience with thru-hiker hunger (a glimpse at Calorie Deficit). By studying your guidebooks you can take advantage of easy, opportunistic food often. These opportunistic stops will also let you order "to go" food for that night or the next day – those pre-packaged noodles can wait another day.

Where there's easy town food to be had, there are hikers.

Do you read food labels? I only just started to, sort of, a few years back. Only a label-dabbler, I could never compete with some of you out there who know glutens, antioxidants and organics. However, in my own way I'm growing and here's why. During my last AT hike, while hiking with this kick-butt athlete of a hiker named LB, she trounced me into the trail with her stamina. Truth be known, many of the best athletes on the AT every season are female. They regularly knock out huge, sunrise-to-sunset days. LB and I hiked about a month together and on several of those days she buried me with her endurance. After a particularly tough day, LB theorized that I wasn't taking in enough carbs. When my shirt started smelling of ammonia, she thought I was going into a form of ketosis (my body was feeding off my muscle rather than my fat, to simplify the definition). So, on one stop in town LB walked the grocery store aisles with me and I started reading labels a bit more in earnest. Since what you eat is your body's fuel, it made a difference and my stamina increased greatly. Good food (good tasting too) doesn't necessarily look appetizing though. That's why those labels become important.

I've recently discovered Larabars, Kind, and Think food bar products. The most hideous looking of the group is the Think Green – Blueberry Noni. I have no idea what the heck a noni is. Of course some of you label aficiona- dos I referenced know exactly what a noni is and can see just how hopeless I am (sigh).

If you're old enough to know what Soylent Green is, well this is what Think Green-Blueberry Noni looked like. Soylent Green was a '70s movie where the old people of the Earth were ground up into energy bars for the younger people to live on during their thru-hikes, only the younger folks didn't know they were eating grandma and grandpa until the end of the movie. Sorry if I just ruined that for those getting ready to Netflix it.

Regardless of how it looks, this Think Green – Blueberry Noni thingy is delicious. Never mind that it's packed with alfalfa grass juice and broccoli powder or that it looks like olive drab, ground up old people. One look and you know if you can get it down it will pay big dividends in stamina on the trail. If only it were sexy looking like a Hostess Cup Cake or a Little Debbie anything. Regardless, both have a place in your hike.

Good food isn't  sexy.

Both help.

Having done taste tests on many energy bars, Power Bar Vanilla and Honey Stinger Peanut Butter Pro are big time yummy to my taste buds. The energy bars that are consistently awful are the healthy bars that try to be chocolate bars - a miserable failure almost always - sort of like polishing a sneaker, it just can't pull off the masquerade.

It may be tantamount to junk food blasphemy to say that a Blueberry Noni is every bit as good as a Hostess cupcake, but remarkably it's true. And the followers of everything organic would also likely view a cupcake comparison to a Think Green Noni bar health food heresy, but so be it. On the trail I live by no food rules other than what tastes good gets eaten, repeatedly and in mass quantities. I am my own man and yes, I like cute Hostess cupcakes and milk chocolate dipped Oreos with my hot cocoa at night. Only a real man could admit this. And quiche! Yes, I love quiche too. There, I said it. Sure I'd love a Grand Marnier Soufflé in the woods if I could, but alas. For the more sophisticated of you, Backpacker's Pantry makes a crème brûlée that only needs a little cold water and three minutes – you could serve it at a dinner party in a pinch.

On my first hike, each maildrop had a small bottle of Captain Morgan Spiced Rum that would get poured into a foldable flask. The challenge was I only allowed myself two swallows per arrival at camp so it would last 'til the next maildrop (even when having luxury items, you want to be conscious of weight). Everything in moderation can add a touch of civilization to the wilderness. However, I've also seen hikers carry a fifth of Jack Daniel's to the trail only to embarrass themselves while ratcheting up their stupidity. Out of control personalities are out on a thru-hike. Thankfully, they are the exception to the genuine, conscientious majority.

Calorie Deficit.

About three weeks into the hike your body will start to change its food needs. This change is called Calorie Deficit. It's the result of 21 or so days burning 5000 to 7000 calories per day that you cannot fully replace. When calorie deficit rears its little head, your hunger will start raging. To understand how this dynamic takes hold of you, I submit a journal entry from my 2006 thru-hike:

"Completed the 12 miles before noon and hitched in for a room at the Budget Inn. The clothes went into the washer then headed across the street for a Whopper with cheese, French-fries and a large Bud. The clothes then went into the dryer, so I went back across the street for a jumbo hot dog, six Krispy-Kreme donuts, large Gatorade and Diet Dr. Pepper. When the clothes were dry and put away, I phoned the local Italian restaurant for Veal Parmesan, salad, bread sticks and a cheesecake. You might think how could anyone be so nuts? And you'd be right... how could I possibly not include a foot-long Italian Sub from Subway when it was just across the parking lot? So I did, and of course some BBQ Fritos. In case of an emergency, a couple of lemon pound cakes were strategically placed in arm's reach on the nightstand."

So that is calorie deficit, and it will join you on your thru-hike. This may seem like bingeing, but, well, maybe it is bingeing. Despite all that eating, I still lost a touch over 50 lbs each thru-hike.

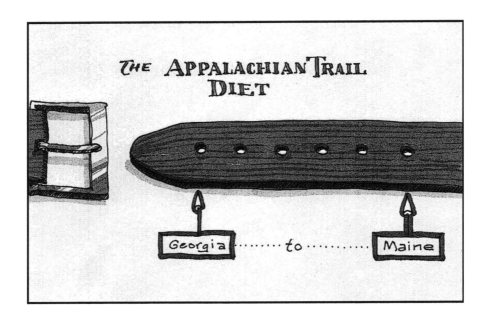

How much weight will you lose?

Since I love soft chocolate chunk cookies, but I hate a chunky waistline and hate the word dieting even more, long-distance backpacking offers a respite from the battle of the bulge.

In addition to my two 2000-Miler patches sewn on my backpack, I also have the Boy Scout "Hiking" Merit Badge that was earned with my youngest nephew, Trevor. In the process of doing one of the required ten-mile hikes, I pulled out some big, soft, chocolate chunk cookies and handed one to him as a surprise/motivation. "Hiking is a good thing to do when you like chocolate chunk cookies," I said.

The body somehow knows that if it experiences prolonged, low-to-moderate activity (notice I did not say exercise), then it knows to go after the fat in our wobbly waddle. Experts call this fat-burning. Do you know what low-to-moderate activity for a long period of time is also called? Thru-hiking! If our activity is high energy, the body goes after the sugars. In one of the truly great gestures in the Grand Plan of Life, deliciously delectable baked goods and hiking happen to be universal opposites. So they cancel each other out – sort of like the marriages of many, judging by the divorce rate.

The long ballyhooed calorie count of the Snickers bar at 250 has rivals with the calorie count of some cookies available along the trail. Discovering that Mrs. Fields Milk Chocolate Chunk Macadamia Nut cookies (which are individually wrapped in a box of eight - making them also ideal for backpacking), deliver an impressive 330 calories with less bulk weight-per-ounce than a Snickers had me giddy during one of my grocery store scavenger hunts.

The joy of eating and the ecstasy of eating sweet lovelies stuffed with big slaps of milk chocolate, white chocolate, or dark chocolate and devouring it whenever the whim hits you has to be one of life's truly great pleasures. Wouldn't it be lovely if the delicacies of the bakeshop were also the most slimming? But alas, such is the curse of the culinary world. In Maine, just before the Hundred-Mile Wilderness, there used to be a home hostel run by The Pie Lady (sadly, retired from the hostel business). When I arrived there on my first hike, I went to the kitchen table, put down a ten (honor system), picked up one of her apple pies and went to my room to eat it joyfully. Yes, the entire pie – free of guilt. And I still lost 50 pounds on my hike! As I mentioned to my nephew, thru-hiking is a great activity if you love eating.

Before you think I'm above weight gain, I am the poster child for post-hike expansion. I will never be skinny. There, I said it. Moving on. But I do love being fit: 2000-mile fit. Despite my propensity for gaining size, I also have a propensity for rapid size loss.

In 2004, I started up The Approach Trail in Georgia with 217 suburban pounds of Belgian waffles, pepperoni pizza and red wine around my middle. Four-and-a-half months later I posed for my summit photo on Mt. Katahdin weighing 163. A shedding of 54 pounds changed my pant waistline of 38 to 34. I hadn't worn a 34 waist since high school. Additionally, that lost weight didn't come at the expense of my athleticism. That thru-hike turned me into a world-class, mountain-climbing machine.

In 2006, the weight loss was about 50 pounds, but I did have a month-long delay while recovering from a broken wrist. More on this later.

If you start the trail more fit, your weight loss will be minimal. If you start the trail with more cityness on you, the weight loss will be more extreme. However, it also seems logical to assume that weight loss will hinge heavily on your pace. If you get up early, hike purpose-fully and continuously throughout the day making good mileage, you'll most likely burn more cityness than, say, a hiker whose trailname is Molasses, Turtle or Sir Naps-Alot.

Even though the longer mileage hiker will have fewer days on the trail, say four to five months, and hence fewer town days of easy eating, the longer daily mileage does seem to translate to greater weight loss. At one time I thought the longer duration hiker who may burn fewer calories each day but has more of them, say six to seven months worth, would lose possibly more weight. But after having seen some comparisons of hikers, I'm not so sure this is true. If you have 30 zero days before reaching Harpers Ferry, chances are you're not going to lose very much.

None of this really matters since an Appalachian Trail thru-hike is more about adventure, escape, and living large than being on a diet program. Weight loss is an obvious fringe benefit though.

Hikers of larger size have lost over 75 pounds routinely if they keep plugging away at the mileage and keep the zero days to a minimum. There's probably a kooky hiking equation that states:

Weight Loss = Daily mileage + Elevation gain + Wind Direction + Pack Weight x Duration – Zero Days, Humidity, Starting Body Weight & Trail Magic.

I do have a tip for those who make New Hampshire and especially Maine in regards to eating. By my own observations and those with whom I've discussed this, every single chance you get to swing into a town to load up on easy town food will be a good strategy. At this point in the journey, the body is straddling a line between a world-class athlete and getting beaten down. Getting big, hearty, extra town food helps replenish your strength both physically and emotionally. Dropping into Gorham, Andover, Stratton, Rangeley, and Monson have all proven beneficial in years past for me. That's just something to store in the memory bank. During my thru-hikes a place called White House Landing in Maine's 100-Mile Wilderness allowed hikers to take a short detour to a floating deck on a lake. With a single air horn blast, the owner would boat ride over and pick you up and a 1 lb burger would get dropped on the grill. But their doors are now closed and their place has been put up for sale. That BIG burger will be missed.

Weightless food.

Before I thru-hike, a visit to my local grocery store must be made. The mission? To explore the aisles of riches, to hunt down foods that are kind to the body, kind to the taste buds and kind to the pack weight. Such a visit will involve an hour of roaming each aisle because you just never know. A few years back I discovered new precooked bacon – fifteen strips of fatty pork that weighed a scant 2 or 3 ounces. I love bacon and can smell it 12 miles from a trail town. No one has a faster hiking pace once my nose locks onto that sizzilin' pig.

Because I find most camp food on the opposite end from culinary bliss, you may falsely think I'm a finicky food baby. Sure, I love steak and chicken and mashed potatoes, but I adore Indian, Mexican, German, Japanese, Cajun, Italian, etc. I've even enjoyed Scotland's haggis (trust me, you don't want to know). Having had most of my lunches at the public school cafeteria growing up, when I say I don't like camp food means it's coming from a palette of taste buds that have a wide spectrum of acceptability.

When you normalize your food bag with some of the flavors not normally found in trail food, you can add so very much. Here are a few that have emerged to deliver the above without loading the pack weight too much.

From those great people who gave us their creamy milk chocolate - the Swiss - we get a staple food that most every hiker carries: cheese. But those blessed Swiss have gone the extra step by thinking of we weight-conscious backpackers. Those alpine geniuses actually put holes in their cheese! Brilliant! The Scandinavians have always been jealous of the Swiss for this – all they ever gave us was ABBA. Who would have thunk it, pre-packaged ultralight cheese?

Donuts aren't necessarily good for the body, but who cares? They're donuts. Besides, they have a big hole in the middle to reduce weight – Another brilliant design.

Of course donut holes might be even lighter since holes weigh nothing because, well, they're holes.

Angel food cake also has a huge hole to reduce its weight, as well as being an air-filled sponge. Angel food cake could most likely be compressed in a compression sack down to the size of a bouillon cube to save space. Although this might need a warning label since popping the angel food cube into your mouth would trigger its quick return to normal size. I can't imagine anyone's mouth able to hold a ten-inch cake, not even a thru-hiker's.

Cheerios and some pastas are hollow and light. Muesli bread is awfully light without using any holes, but it's awfully awful.

When hiking out of town with bread, I usually will have lifted all the choices on the shelf to find the one with the lightest touch. Even though I want the taste of bread, I still don't want to carry one that approaches the load of a holiday fruitcake. The new mini bagels not only sport a hole, but their diminutive size makes them space saving and a candidate for our consideration. Pitted olives are holey but who wants a big tub of olives after a 20-mile day?

Serendipity.

So clearly I'm having fun here with all this food analysis. However, there is a clear winner for a food that meets the standards of good calories, carbs, protein, is light in weight and delivers great taste for emotional strength. The award goes to...TRAIL MAGIC!

Yes, it's light (you don't carry it), it's good since it's a surprise and a gift all in one. No space in your pack is required and most of all, it's free! Trail Magic will broaden your smile and may find you in serendipitous moments. I've seen it as 5-gallon buckets hanging from trees. I've seen it as discreetly placed coolers filled with iced-down fruit juices. Even boldly conspicuous coolers with chairs for lingering. For those who make it north to Vermont, one chilly stream has had a wire corral of sodas for years of hiker seasons.

Trail Magic should never be expected, never be confused for an entitlement. It is and has always been a gift provided by the generosity and money of others. Be it a soda or full-blown breakfast with all the extras. Many who cannot hike themselves like to remain involved with the texture of the Appalachian Trail thru-hiking season by giving back, passing forward a good deed they themselves once received or being a bright spot in an arduous day. All we hikers have to do is be appreciative for even the smallest gesture.

The first Trail Magic that found me took place two weeks into the hike where the AT crosses a busy parking lot called Newfound Gap in the Great Smoky Mountains National Park. During my rest break there, a man asked if I was thru-hiking. Hearing the answer, he handed me a 12-inch roast beef and cheddar sub. Out of the clear blue yonder, a complete stranger (now turned Trail Angel) wanted to pass forward the many kindnesses he had received during his thru-hike years earlier. It was delicious and only reaffirmed that every meal didn't have to be traditional trail food.

Trail Magic can also be quite large in its generosity. While passing through a notoriously tough section of New York known as The Agony Grind, Trail Angels had left their phone number, along with Trail Magic if any thru-hikers needed assistance. That particular week had been very difficult with the excessive heat wave, and this area is water-challenged to begin with. It didn't help that I'd just had a horrific Timber Rattlesnake encounter. I was frazzled and feeling a bit desperate. When they answered their phone, they could hear it in my voice and were there in 15 minutes to pick me up. Since the only motel a town over no longer welcomed hikers, they invited me, a complete stranger, to spend the night at their home. While showering the trail off, they did my laundry and pulled a nice dinner together. The rest of the evening was sharing stories, watching baseball and eating ice cream. Thanks to their kindness during a very low moment, I regained my emotional strength by the next morning.

A year later, they'd go to their mailbox to find a copy of my first book. In it they found a special tribute to their Trail Angel evening with me.

My Maildrop list.

These destinations may or may not still be valid. Do your own homework and confirm locations with up-to-date guidebooks before adapting. Sometimes locations change ownership and no longer accept maildrops. Where only a specific delivery carrier is spelled out, I've tried to point them out. I suggest that on every maildrop you clearly print "Hold for AT hiker: your real name" on each box. When the location is a place to stay, I point that out as well, so the owners know my intentions before I arrive. An example of that: "Hold for AT hiker and future guest: your real name".

Whomever you entrust with the mail-out responsibilities, know that packages should be mailed out <u>a full two weeks before your estimated time of arrival.</u> Some of these rural locations take a bit longer for mail to get to than places in the city. It's quite frustrating to arrive and find that your maildrop isn't there, forcing you to sit around and wait. This can be avoided by keeping the keepers of your packages informed of your pace every week. Often, I'd tell my folks – who took care of my maildrops - to move all my dates up a week due to my making better progress than anticipated. (We do tend to turn ourselves into mile-making athletes.) I've also added in some opportunistic places to stay along the way, but they are not necessarily a maildrop. The goal with this list is to reduce the weight one must carry. It will be rare that you'll ever carry more than six days of food on your journey. These small towns' United States Post Offices along the trail have limited hours though. Be sure to keep this in mind for pickups.

Box 1   Walasi-Yi Center
             12471 Gainesville Hwy
             Blairsville, GA 30512

Box 2   Hiawassee Budget Inn
             193 S. Main St
             Hiawassee, GA 30546 (Guests only, UPS only)

Box 3   Nantahala Outdoor Center
             13077 Hwy 19W
             Bryson City, NC 28713 (USPS, UPS & Fed Ex)

Box 4   Your Real Name c/o General Delivery
             Fontana Dam, NC 28733 (Closed Fri – Sun)

Box 5   Standing Bear Farm
             4255 Green Corner Rd
             Hartford, TN 37753

Box 6   Bluff Mountain Outfitters
             152 Bridge St PO Box 114
             Hot Springs, NC 28743

Box 7   Nolichucky Hostel
             151 River Rd
             Erwin, TN 37650

Box 8   Kincora Hiker Hostel
             1278 Dennis Cove Rd
             Hampton, TN 37658

Box 9   Mt. Rogers Outfitters
             110 Laurel Ave

PO Box 546

Damascus, VA 24236

Box 10   The Relax Inn

7253 Lee Hwy

Rural Retreat, VA 24368

(Accepts for guests only)

Box 11   Holiday Motor Lodge

401 N Main St

Pearisburg, VA 2413 (Accepts maildrops)

Box 12   Howard Johnson Express Inn

437 Roanoke Rd

Daleville, VA 2408

(Accepts for registered guests)

Box 13   Your Name c/o General Delivery

Buena Vista, VA 24416

Box 14   Your Name c/o General Delivery

Waynesboro, VA 22980 (Closed Saturday)

(Various Shenandoah N. P. Camp Stores and Lodges)

Box 15   Your Name c/o General Delivery

Front Royal, VA 22630

Box 16   Your Name c/o General Delivery

Harpers Ferry, WVA 25425

Box 17   Rite Spot Motel/Scottish Inns

5651 Lincoln Way East

Fayetteville, PA 17222 (Accepts for guest

past years)

Box 18   Your Name c/o General Delivery

Boiling Springs, PA 17007

(Mon – Sat, limited hours)

Box 19   Your Name c/o General Delivery

Port Clinton, PA 19549

(Mon – Sat, limited hours)

Box 20   Your Name c/o General Delivery

Delaware Water Gap, PA 18327

Box 21   Your Name c/o General Delivery

Bear Mtn, NY 10911

(Limited hours, closed Sat, Sun)

(Glamping begins – Kent, Sharon, Salisbury, Great Barrington food fest and motels)

Box 22   Your Name c/o General Delivery

Kent, CT 06757

Box 23   Your Name c/o General Delivery

Dalton, MA 01226

(Mt. Greylock summit/Bascom Lodge is a great place to stay in a thunderstorm)

Box 24   The Mountain Goat

4886 Main St

Manchester Center, VT 05255

(US 4/The Inn at Long Trail & Pub has great food and relaxing. And laundry!)

Box 25 Your Name c/o General Delivery
Hanover, NH 03755
(Welcome to The Whites – Gulp!)

Box 26 Your Name c/o General Delivery
North Woodstock, NH 03262

Box 27 The Hikers Welcome Hostel
1396 NH 25
Glencliff, NH 03238
(USPS via PO Box 25, UPS & FedEx)

Box 28 AMC Highland Center
Route 302
Bretton Woods, NH 03575
(Shuttle - Webster Cliffs/AT)

(Joe Dodge Lodge at Pinkham Notch)

Box 29 Your Name c/o General Delivery
Gorham, NH 03581

Box 30 Pine Ellis Hiking Lodge
20 Pine St
PO Box 12
Andover, ME 04216

Box 31 Your Name c/o General Delivery
Stratton, ME 04982

Box 32 Your Name c/o General Delivery
Monson, ME 04464

(Abol Bridge Camp Store at beginning of Baxter State Park)

Box 33   Appalachian Trail Lodge and Cafe

33 Penobscot Ln

Millinocket, ME 04462 (Accepts for guests)

As you can see, there are many places that accept mail-drops other than just the US Post Office. This streamlines the resupply chores each town stop. I, for one, have never felt that swinging off the trail for my maildrops ever cramped my freedom or escape; you may feel the opposite before you start. But once you settle in to knocking out miles, some creature comforts of town, even just a swing by the Post Office (and, of course, a visit to a diner) always lifted up my adventurous spirit.

You may even create fond trail experiences as I did when I went into Barrington, Vermont for my maildrop for my third pair of shoes. While standing in a line with six Towner's at the Post Office, I loudly offered a public apology for my aroma, that I was hiking the Appalachian Trail. Laughter broke out from everyone, as did inquiries, making the necessary chore memorable. After a visit for a real town breakfast, I was still able to make the 18.7 miles to my night's destination.

Items found in my maildrops were a disposable razor for a clean up. My next section's map profiles and data pages. Spare AAA batteries. A clean, new gallon Ziploc for trash. All my food – dinners, breakfast milkshake powders, Fritos and goodies. Firestarters. On my first thru, each box had a small bottle of Captain Morgan Spiced Rum. Small travel shampoo. Pre-addressed and stamped envelopes for my drawings and journal entries

- I went old school and did not carry a phone for uploads. My GNC Mega Man vitamins, extra Excedrin and Tylenol PM for bedtime. So, a mixture of stuff.

Maildrops do require you to plan them out before you start. Fill the boxes with the appropriate foods and supplies and create a schedule. Your miles, as outlined in a dynamic I call The Circle in the next section, will determine how many maildrops you choose and how often you resupply.

Titanium Spork helps

Ice cream can be rock hard from an opportunistic convenience store freezer. A titanium spork means not having to wait for your favorite flavor to soften – an agonizing ten minutes with a lesser, plastic one.

Secret

Making miles is your "job".

Do you know how far you can walk? Unless you have some experience with either long-distance backpacking, charity walk-a-thon's or forgetting where you parked your car at the mall, how could you?

Discovering how far you can walk is always one of the fun discoveries of the journey, especially when it's not along a highway with an empty gas container. Whether it's 10 miles, 15, 20 or more, setting a new personal best has both tangible and intangible benefits during a thru-hike. You'll discover far more than the distance: you'll discover that it's not such a small world after all.

My first job out of college took me to New York City – a place where walking is common. For the first time in my life, I walked holes into the soles of my penny loafers. Obviously, when one walks holes in one's loafers, the walker is the farthest thing from being called a Loafer - nor do these shoes cost a penny but rather a pretty penny.

Walking is one of the best aspects of New York City. I walked everywhere using the technique of "follow the green lights," so you're constantly zig zagging to make progress, shortening the time from point A to B. Walking had practical benefits since my first job as an Assistant Art Director in advertising paid a whopping 12K a year, thus taxis were a last option to subways. Fortunately, I got overtime, which was a huge error on my employer's part – my first year I grossed nearly triple my starting salary. This paid for extravagant luxuries like eating and shoe repair.

When you start walking (on purpose that is) the very idea of using your feet to go way the heck over yonder is quite remarkable. Said differently, thru-hiking is walking from horizon to horizon, and it leads to all sorts of things you aren't prepared for. The slowness of foot travel seems to reintroduce us to the idea of having patience.

Our world has become frenetic to such a high level that gigabytes whiz by our eyes and ears without our conscious Self able to grasp it all. Our subconscious, however, doesn't miss a thing. The result is tight shoulders, short attention spans and road rage. You can experience the feeling that you're always behind, which may explain why seemingly everyone behind the wheel is speeding. Many may also feel like they're always reacting rather than seeing the bigger picture.

Traveling at foot-speed lets you know that indeed there is time, that indeed the world is still big and it's OK to not multitask every tick of the second hand. You might find that you won't become less of a person if you let that driver merge lanes in front of you. Traveling at foot-speed and the patience required in walking those miles will be one of the huge acclimations in a thru-hike. Having witnessed it first-hand, I can assure you that if you can let go of the suburban go-go and settle into the simplicity of single-tasking and the pace of walking, you'll discover a true liberation and reordering of priorities.

In a blog post by T.D. Wood on walking he writes:

"Walking, ideally, is a state in which the mind, the body, and the world are aligned, as though they were three characters finally in conversation together, three notes suddenly making a chord. Walking allows us to be in our bodies and in the

world without made busy by them. It leaves us free to think without being wholly lost in our thoughts."

"The rhythm of walking generates a kind of rhythm of thinking, and the passage through a landscape echoes or stimulates the passage through a series of thoughts. This creates an odd consonance between internal and external passage, one that suggests the mind is also a landscape of sorts and that walking is one way to traverse it."

Thank you, Mr. Wood, for putting that so well.

Years ago, my pet peeve was getting a coffee puddle on the saucer when ordering in a restaurant – the mug has eliminated this greatest of travesties. Now, after 5000 miles of single-tasking, my pet peeve is how people can't do anything without a cell-phone stuck to their head. It's easy to observe someone driving with one hand on the wheel and the other up by their ear, at times this posture happens as they back out of their own drive-ways (what, you couldn't call before you drove?). Having barely avoided two mishaps with others that had paying attention while driving as a second priority, I suppose I'm venting. Multitasking has become habitual in suburbia.

I freely admit that the pressure in business to do more with less or the orchestration of family life with work life imposes time pressure on everyone. Multitasking while driving, though, often leads to the injury of you or others, which leads to court dates. Multitasking in back-packing often leads to a hike-ending injury. Whether it's our growing impatience that makes us believe we must constantly multitask or the multitasking that has created the impatience, who knows?

Walking introduces us to purity. Its very action is single-minded. The farther we walk the deeper the impression burrows into us. Couple this with birdsong, mountain breezes, the scent of evergreen and a wilderness of awe and you'll wonder how walking fell out of favor. When you haven't walked to get where you're going for a while, you almost question if you're allowed to do it. In my part of the country, there's only a sidewalk on one side of the street and no sidewalk leading out of the neighborhood. Today when we see someone walking we think poverty, suspended license. Seldom do we think energy conscious, enlightened, thru-hiker. One of the mental barriers to walking I had to step over was that it was indeed OK to go for a walk or try to walk a great distance. Then once I did start walking again, a simple curiosity existed within me: about how far could I walk?

Routinely my neighbors drive three houses down the street to visit one another, so walking 8 miles or 18 would be out of their scope of imagination. Once you clear this mental hurdle you may start pondering, as I did, what you're capable of doing. Do you have a 20-miler in you?

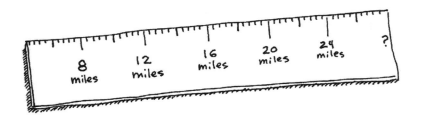

Once you experience the pride in doing such a distance, a peak experience for sure, curiosity of a 25- and 30-mile day emerge. For me, the pride in doing them day after day is empowering. Where taking one's time with a casual saunter has its benefits, so does the accomplishment of taking on bigger mileage to alleviate our distance insecurities. Arming us with knowledge that we can hike long if needed gives the hiker options with camp, town visits, and number of days out before resupply. This latter point will be crucial in determining pack weight loads in a dynamic I call "The Circle", which as I've stated will be discussed later.

There's a fun phrase out on the trail that slower hikers like to embrace as a way of countering all the youth and athleticism of others who crank out bigger mileage days. The expression is, "Last one to Katahdin is the winner." Something you need to understand is that no one cares about your miles except you. Your trailname can be Rocket or Pokey, but I assure you there is always someone faster or slower. Countless others remind us that it's not the destination, but the journey that is important. For whatever reason, the AT has recently seen several speed hikers. (Some aren't really hiking so much as running.) Some out there are impressed by the amazingly short time they do it in. I am not one of those. Supported (hiking with a team that meets you along the journey with food and shelter) or unsupported (where you're fully self-supported) records of speed where the land is a blur - I fail to see the value (sigh). My thru-hikes changed me. They gave me my patience back because I spent time savoring the journey. Hike your own hike, as the saying goes.

I'm a big fan of a good mileage day, whether or not it's a personal best, because of the empowerment it provides the hiker. It is unfortunate that some turn these long distances into unappealing displays of bragging rather than towards quiet pride. Your distance doesn't define you as a person, and someone who does greater mileage than you doesn't make them the better hiker. The point here is how mileage, when achieved, can benefit the individual. The day I did my first 30-miler (34.1 to be exact) I wasn't spent, downtrodden by day's end. I was up, bubbly, master of my universe. From the time I did my first 20, then a 25, 28 or 34, I provided myself with an inner power that just couldn't be bought. To acquire this sensation may be the best reason for doing a big day (other than bacon and burgers and fried chicken and cakes, pies, fresh fruit and vegetables from arriving in the next town).

To empower yourself with a good mileage day is to stand a bit taller, to carry your shoulders a tad more square – it'll be like drinking a confidence elixir. Distance-accomplishment is just another way to shore up, even elevate your emotional strength during a long-distance hike. Certainly there are plenty of things outside your control that will conspire to erode it.

Don't define yourself by someone else's mileage or plan…unless you want to. Sometimes you'll get inspired by others to push your own distance envelope, to achieve a new personal best. However, don't for a minute believe you're less of a hiker if your mileage is less. Each hiker has a different motivation and each motivation can wane. My first year I met a hiker who averaged 31 miles a day in the first month but didn't succeed. I've met hikers who've had 40-mile days back to back and

I know one who did a 52! The point is there is always someone faster, slower, has bigger mileage, whatever. It works for them, it may not work for you.

One day you'll meet someone new and before you know it you're pushing yourself for the fun of it. In '04, during my first thru-hike, I met Goose. Being younger with better fitness, he was covering about 20 miles a day. Inspired and feeling more fit in the second month when we met, I started joining Goose in his planned mileage for a couple of weeks. Sometimes described as a "push pull," I matched his distance, which resulted in a surge of about 4 to 6 miles farther than what I was averaging. What may be normal for one hiker may be a new personal best for another. I chose to step up to another level of distance because it brought me pride to do so, thus I was still Hiking My Own Hike. Goose inspired me to see what more I could achieve, he just pulled me along whether he knew it or not. During my second thru-hike, my mileage inspired others around me to match my pace. That thru-hike saw me cover 486 miles through Virginia in just 24 days, completing all 550 miles of that state in one month. I took two Zeros (no miles on the AT, "taking a day off" to rest), five Neros (near-zero days - which meant lower mileage - were closer to being half-days that ended with me hitching into a town for the night) and stopped to smelled the evergreen often. As the days get longer - if you'll get up and get going early - 20 miles by late afternoon will be well within the range of most hikers. Here's what that period looked like in daily miles:

"26 Days"

19.0 Miles →	22.2 →	25.3 →	25.7 →
0	18.5 →	23.6 →	25.1 →
10.9 (Half day)	21.9 →	23.4 →	11.3 (Half day)
20.0 →	21.3 →	20.4 →	20.6 →
26.5 →	23.4 →	17.5 →	12.0 (Half day)
0	22.9 →	25.1 →	10.8 (Half day)
31.2 →	8.1 (Half day)		

If tenacity allows you to reach The Whites of New Hampshire, you'll understand why there's the saying "80% of the journey is complete but only 20% of the effort." Gone are the switchbacks. Fifteen-hundred to 2000 foot climbs become 2000 to 3500 foot climbs routinely. The shelter of a tree canopy is replaced by above-treeline exposure to fast moving weather events. Mountain breezes can ramp up to hurricane force winds that can take you off your feet. As beautiful and as breathtaking as the area of The Whites is, its week-long passage always gave me a touch of anxiety. Surrounded by all this grandeur yet knowing that fine weather can quickly turn dramatic if caught on a ridgeline never let me truly relax. Hopefully your passage will.

The strenuous climbs turned my normal 20+ mile days to low teens. Where some climbs down south might take 1 to 2 hours, climbs here can start in the morning with summits not reached 'til early afternoon. Latitude-wise, you're higher on the hemisphere, so even though it may be July or August, the temps are cooler and the nights require your warmer clothing and sleeping bag you began with. It snows every month of the year and people routinely need search and rescue and even die from exposure; warning signs let all who hike there know the sobering realities. During my second passage I handled the frets better. When a few days of bad weather would come storming in on the Franconia Ridge section, I wisely waited it out in North Woodstock. This is one of the most spectacular ridge walks of the entire journey, so having good weather for it will be one of the hike's highlights.

By the time you reach The Whites you are a mountain climbing athlete. For it to suddenly pull down everyone's miles tells you the level of difficulty. When I did a post-hike assessment of the top ten climbs on a northbound journey, not surprisingly half were in The White Mountains of New Hampshire. Here is my list in David Letterman backward style:

10. **The Approach Trail, Georgia, because it's the first climb.**

9. **Blood Mountain, Georgia,**

8. **Roan Mountain, North Carolina**

7. **Three Ridges Mountain, Virginia**

6. **Mt. Washington, New Hampshire**

5. **Mt. Lincoln/Mt. Lafayette, New Hampshire**

4. **Mt. Mooselauke, New Hampshire**

3. **Peak E, The Wildcats, New Hampshire**

2. **South Peak, Mt. Kinsman, New Hampshire**

1. **Mt. Katahdin, Maine, The Greatest Mountain**

So, back to the opening question – Do you know how far you can walk? Do you want to know? Do you even care to know? The Appalachian Trail's starting plaque states, "For those who seek fellowship with the wilderness." Still valid, most definitely, but the mantra heard more frequently today is, "Hike your own hike." Seek the wilderness. Hike short. Hike long. Hike colossal. Only do it for the sake of your own joy. What will you discover this year about yourself? Why not take a walk and find out just how proud of yourself you can be?

The Circle.

There's a dynamic in thru-hiking, frankly in all backpacking, that connects mileage, food and pack weight. I've named it The Circle. Each influences the other in a loop. Here's how it works:

1) Your daily mileage will have an influence on your food needs before your next resupply.

2) Your food needs will have an influence on your pack weight.

3) Your pack weight will have an influence on your daily mileage.

You can easily factor in terrain and weather to #1 (your mileage), and opportunistic food to #2 (diners and such) as well as adding your water weight and the weight of your footwear to #3, the weight your body must carry.

Understanding The Circle can help you tackle your journey. Let's consider, for instance, that your next resupply or maildrop is 60 miles away. If you hike 10-mile days, you'll need six days of food for your six-day journey, which at 2 pounds of food per day (on average) would mean 12 pounds worth of food you'll be carrying on day one. If, however, you're willing to hike 15-mile days, you'll arrive at the same 60-mile destination in four days. Four days journey means carrying 8 pounds of food (2 pounds per day), a savings of 4 pounds every time you pick up your left leg and every time you pick up your right leg. Everyone with me? ...Good. On average, hikers will take 2000 steps per mile. So by avoiding those 4 pounds every time you pick up your legs (because of a willingness to do 15-mile days rather than 10), you avoid carrying 120,000 lbs on that first day. Here's the math:

2000 steps per mile for 15 miles = 30,000 steps.

30,000 steps without 4 pounds of food per step =

120,000 lbs

not carried, not schlepped, not tolerated.

How many of us think our smile might be a tad wider if we weren't carrying 120,000 pounds? Not only will this help your disposition, but also your legs will have less fatigue, and you'll have more energy that can help manage a climb or result in a quicker pace. This means an earlier arrival at camp for longer rest. Less fatigue may also help with trips and falls where you simply don't lift your leg high enough. Amazingly, it doesn't stop on day one. Each day in the 60 mile section will allow you to avoid carrying 120,000 pounds. How much more fresh will you be reaching that destination on day four, having avoided nearly a half-million pounds?

Now add that week to the next and the next and the odds of a joyful journey get better, don't they? Turn those weeks into months and, wow, what a difference in the grind of a thru-hike. So a willingness to make mileage is also a strategic way to avoid excessive weight carrying. Factor this dynamic with others (such as gear selection) to reduce the burden of weight your body must tolerate and you'll climb and stride at a higher level.

Daily mileage choreography.

Finding a hiking rhythm that agrees with you will bring some control to the grind of making miles. Listed below are six primary mileage strategies that Thru-hikers use daily – some hikers staying strictly to one, others using all six during the same hike.

1) Hike to the shelter locations as your mileage strategy, thus moving from shelter to shelter. Some days

you may hike to the third shelter in your day. Other days it may be to the fourth. This provides easy water sources, sometimes a privy, a community of others and picnic tables at which to cook and eat. I discovered this strategy on my first hike when I was more of a scaredy-cat. Anchoring myself to the shelters each night seemed to give me a greater sense of security. I'm not alone in thinking this. Staying at one of the 250 shelters of the AT makes you feel you're not completely in the wilderness, not completely vulnerable.

2) Hike to a set time in the day and then stealth camp. This will provide you with less mayhem from others at the shelters and add richness to the wilderness adventure. When you choose this strategy, you'll want to gather water before your designated time so when a nice flat spot is located, you stop and call it home for the night.

3) Hike to a shelter location near the end of the day, get water, cook, eat, visit with others and then pack up and continue on an hour or so. When a nice spot in the woods is found, just pitch the tent, crawl in the sleeping bag and drift off. I found this to agree with me on my second hike, as my forest acclimation no longer had me jumping at every strange sound in the darkness. It was during this time that my hike was at its most liberating and free.

4) Go shorter on your mileage the first day back out of town. Your resupply pack weight will be at its heaviest.

5) Go long into town since your pack food weight will have been eaten (about 2 lbs per day). The miles will fly by with a lighter load. This allowed me to enjoy town food that night and the next if I was zeroing there. It does cost more to do this, but going long expands your fitness envelope, turning you quicker into a Super You.

6) Go short into town (a Nero – a near zero day) to save on expenses. You hike to a spot near the town or road and camp or shelter there. The next morning you do a few miles and hitch in. This still gives you the entire day in town to manage chores – laundry, resupply, maildrop pick-up, grocery shop and visit the local restaurants to eat yourself silly, then head back out. It also allows you to grab a motel room or hostel bunk for the night before heading back out tomorrow.

Become a single-tasker.

A story I often recount is how one hiker was moving along the trail nicely and decided to change the music she was enjoying on that bright day. Whether wanting to be efficient or just getting sloppy, she focused on her music device while still walking, unaware that the AT took a small turn - a short, side trail to a vista over-look that continued straight. Focused on finding a radio station rather than staying in the moment, she was hiking towards the vista cliff. Finding a clear station with music that pleased her, she finally looked up and saw she was only a step from plummeting off a 15-foot cliff.

It's easy to get sloppy over the long period of time of a thru-hike, but your well-being and the success of your adventure depend on your ability to stay focused. It could be walking up on a sun-warming timber rat-tler, missing a black bear sighting, or not seeing a dou-ble-blaze that signifies to stay alert - a turn is imminent or another trail is crossing.

Instead of multitasking, a wiser course would be to stop, focus on finding the music station, then start walking again when you can stay in that moment. Imagine pull-ing on a shirt over your head as you walk down a stair-case. It may be efficient, but it's hardly wise. Believe me, the AT doesn't need any help at taking you down.

Resist the habit of multitasking during your hike. When you walk, walk. When you adjust your iPod, adjust your iPod.

Although the AT may have 80,000 white blazes (estimates vary) to keep you found, not paying attention has gotten hikers lost. Just after crossing the first state line of Georgia into North Carolina, the trail takes an uncharacteristic abrupt hard right on a northbound direction. However, that well-worn pathway also has an abrupt left turn, equally well worn. One hiker went left and was lost for three days until a Forest Ranger found him, shaken and distraught after he reported himself lost by phone. One quickly learns that there are two powerful triggers to anxiety in the backcountry: 1) Not knowing where you are and 2) Darkness is coming; the first usually triggers the second. One does not need a compass on the AT. A map or guidebook, yes, but not a compass. It may be the most well-marked trail in the world. Embrace single-tasking and you stay found.

Is moving Northbound uphill?

It seems so, doesn't it? If you gain in latitude, doesn't "gain" mean going up? If north is at the top of the globe and south the bottom, doesn't that also prove that a northbound hike means always climbing? If you look at a map of the United States, aren't you always ascending from Georgia to Maine?

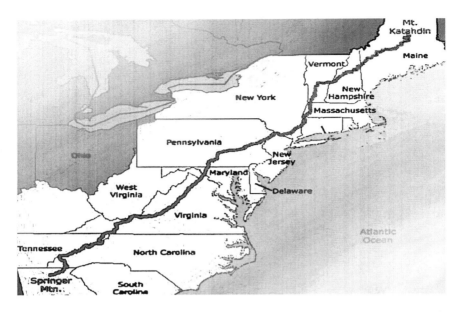

It sure seems like it. Plenty of non-hiking types think this as well. Countless times, a Towner trying to be cute will cackle, "I'd hike south if I were you. That's downhill." I try to be polite, but a few times my retort has been less so, "Yea thanks, and remember your meds need periodic adjustment with your doctor. Enjoy your day." That usually gets a puzzled stare.

Of course, many of you who don't hike or are new to it always feel that hiking south would indeed be walking downhill. Come on, admit it. It can be a challenging mental issue early on, that is until tread touches trail. I can assure you it's only a perception. Moving north on the AT can actually be downhill and moving south can be uphill – nutty isn't it? Let's not even talk about how moving northbound is often moving east or west or even south at times. Occasionally moving south means moving in every direction other than south. It can be psychologically puzzling early in a hike, say in the Nantahala Wilderness area where you turn east, then west then south – this feels like the most "bass ackwards" way of getting to Maine. It's also why a compass isn't required so much as paying attention to the white-blazes that mark the trail. This is also why it is referred to as hiking "northbound" or "southbound", rather than the true direction of north or south.

Since hiking trails are not highways (and without the same budgets to plow through mountains, thank goodness), they wiggle around the topography of the land (and property lines) to find their route. As a result, this thing called the Appalachian Trail at times looks nothing like an idyllic, storybook trail of well-worn pathway through a forest that's so easy to visualize. Acknowledged as the toughest of America's three long-distance trails (The Pacific Crest and Continental Divide Trail's being the other two), the AT sends its followers periodically up rock scree, across boulder fields and through collapsed granite labyrinths that resemble fallen Jenga games rather than meandering footpaths.

I read an absurd Trailjournals.com entry once where a newish hiker claimed the AT was poorly marked! Poorly marked!? You mean 80,000 painted white blazes, about one every 30 steps and a well-worn path in the forest wasn't clear enough? Jeez, I guess you can't please everyone – I suppose all the other trails they hiked had velvet ropes lining the pathway? There are Interstate Highways not as well marked as the Appalachian Trail. In fact, at just about any point over 14 states, one can stop and look either northbound or southbound and see a white blaze. Many may even think it's over white-blazed.

On an up note, moving north does seem to be a positive, optimistic thing to do. "I'm heading north," sounds uplifting, that you've got your act together. And it certainly sounds a bit more reassuring than acknowledging to others, "I'm heading south," or, "I'm going downhill." Yikes, that doesn't sound good, does it? So heading north, although it sounds more difficult, is not without its emotional benefits.

This of course does not mean that going north is a continuous descent; heading northbound does mean going uphill quite frequently. But, who goes up must also come down, so there is plenty of downhill too.

Of course, many of you think going downhill (physically, not emotionally) is much easier, right? It certainly can be at times, but it can also be one of the more painful kinds of hiking, since gravity will force your entire body and pack weight into attacking your knees (or toes, if shoes are the wrong size). So all that weight is attacking each knee individually, and that doesn't even take into account the inertia of your body mass.

Since mountains are by definition tall objects, gravity will heighten all that weight on every irritating downhill step, attacking our knees. The worst, though, are the rock staircases masterfully crafted by many of the skilled trail maintenance crews of the AT. The staircases are marvels of engineering that use nature's building blocks – boulders- and they're diabolical at dialing up the knee pain. Many a hiker who'd fret the uphills early on because of their leg-busting, lung-heaving demands will flop their opinion to preferring them once they discover the agony of the knees by going the "easy" direction of downhill.

Honing your trail legs.

Just like staying in the moment to prevent what can happen from happening, certain walking habits can also contribute to your well-being and stepping prowess. You'll encounter a broad texture of terrain and obstacles, so here are some helpful techniques.

Step over.

When a tree falls in the forest, not only does it make a thundering crash, occasionally it lands straight across the trail. Referred to as a "blowdown", whether it was blown down or not, it obstructs a clean passage of the AT. Before a trail maintenance crew can solve or reduce its impact, there are ways to minimize its impact on you.

When faced with these blowdowns, the tendency is to step up onto them and then step down. Avoid that. In a thru-hike, that means a whole lot more unnecessary impacts to your knees, and impacts add up after weeks and months. Instead of stepping up, consider the simple act of stepping over. Simple, right? To step over obstacles and avoid at least some downward impacts might be the difference in avoiding knee issues. When the fallen tree's girth is so large that a step over isn't possible, a sit and spin of the legs to the other side keeps you moving. Hikers in front of you may have already blazed a detour path around some blowdowns if they are too large to step over or too branchy to sit and spin onto. Follow the path of least resistance.

Step deep

When climbing a rocky ascent of boulders, step deep to the mountainside of the boulder rather than placing your foot on the front edge. No matter how large, boulders can teeter. If so, your tread may slip off, possibly slamming a knee into said boulder. (Assorted expletives and one gimpy knee result. Not good.) By stepping deep on the climb and stepping shallow on the descent (the mountainside), you reduce or even eliminate a teeter surprise. If the teeter surprise isn't in play it could be the slippery surprise from wetness. Keeping your steps tighter to the mountainside and away from the edges is a wise habit to embrace.

Those of us who have snowy/icy winters learn that by shortening our stride and taking smaller steps, we keep our legs tighter underneath our center of gravity. The same is true for many of the conditions faced on the wet wood and wet stone of the Appalachian Trail. Both wet surfaces can literally be as slippery as black ice, and shortening your stride will help you keep your footing. I'm sure you'll forget about this warning of how incredibly slippery wet wood can be - that is until you put your foot on it. Once you slip and land on your butt then you'll suddenly remember this technique.

As you move farther north to the Mid-Atlantic states, you will routinely come across split-log and plank walkways. They are found in areas prone to flooding and they continue off-and-on all the way to Maine. Fortunately, most of those have chain- sawed grooves and crosshatches to offer some modest grip. But any wet wood in a forest presents slippery challenges, even if man made. Some of this wet wood are trail maintenance, rain management runoff logs half buried – these can be as slippery as black ice, too. Avoid placing your foot on them and step elsewhere. Sadly, people die on the AT every year due to a whole host of reasons, at times from slipping and hitting their head.

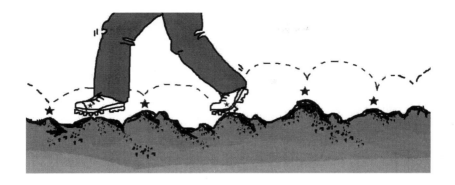

Another stepping technique that can smooth out the less-than-smooth rocky trail is the Top-to-Top. Rather than the slower process of placing your foot in between every rock and all the leg lifting required, one places each footstep on the higher points of the rocks in front of you. This top-of-the-rock to the next top-of-the-rock technique can have you pass through an awkward section without slowing your pace. Patches of rocks will appear constantly, and by using the Top-to-Top technique, you can exit the other end of these nuisances with nary a pause. As in all stepping techniques, your passage requires concentration, staying in the moment, and staying within your abilities. Honing your trail legs will be a daily event. Each section and each state will present new levels of awkward footing, but as with anything you practice, you'll begin to move through these areas with the sureness of a Ninja. You won't have to so much think as let your newly honed instincts flow. I'd say it's not too dissimilar to a piano player - if you think too much then the rhythm of the melody will be choppy. Once you discover your trail legs, the journey picks up speed and daily miles multiply with less effort.

To pole or not to pole?

An additional consideration in keeping your feet underneath you is employing trekking (or hiking, if you prefer) poles, one in each hand. In a stroke of luck they're sold in pairs!

(For those of you inclined to wear boots because you don't want a turned ankle, only something like a well-placed tree or possibly a trekking pole will stop that lateral movement. High boots offer ankles more stability, but do not make you immune to turned ankles.)

Years ago before I started my first thru-hike I was pondering this same question. About an hour away at an REI, I heard of a Thru-hiker who'd be answering questions one Saturday. So off I went to seek an answer, if not an opinion. The Thru-hiker admitted that he didn't have trekking poles for the first 450 miles to Damascus, Virginia, but bought them and wished he'd had had them the entire way. Well, that seemed pretty clear – I've used trekking poles on both my hikes and probably fell less as a result.

Trekking poles are about having more contact points with the ground for improved balance and stability over the rough and awkward terrain – remember you've got a suitcase on your back. They also reduce the attacks to your knees on the step-downs while lowering the odds of falling or turning an ankle.

In backpacking you are going to fall. Sometimes you'll fall hard. Sometimes you'll fall soft. But you'll fall less frequently when you have a trekking pole in each hand, and you'll lower the odds of injury that goes beyond just a turned ankle.

First and foremost, there are really only three things to know about trekking poles.

1) To determine the proper height for your pole, just loosen the shaft locks - either quick release lever locks or the older twisting camber locks - then lengthen the poles so that when you're holding the grip, your arm forms a 90-degree bend at the elbow. Then retighten your locks. Now, when you stand holding the pole, your forearm is parallel to the ground.

2) How to hold the straps is a little trickier. When properly used, straps can become tools that assist in both ascending and descending mountains. Unfortunately, we all have just enough ego that we can't imagine there's a wrong way to employ a strap. As the illustrations point out, you enter the strap from underneath (A), bringing it to your wrist. Next, you allow the strap to lay <u>inside</u> your palm (B) before grabbing the grip. With the strap inside the palm and while holding the grip your thumb (C) will be over one side of the strap, and you'll now have complete control of the pole whether you're holding the grip or not. Amazing, but true. There should be

no sloppiness to the strap loop - it should be close fitting, resulting in better control.

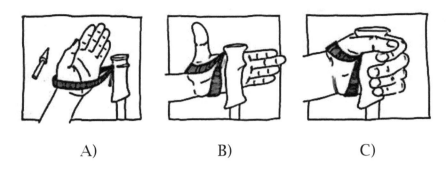

A)   B)   C)

This affords you the luxury to release the grip when awkward angles make it tough on our anatomy's limitations (down mountains and step-downs). This is the same strap configuration that is also used in cross-country or Nordic skiing, allowing you to slightly let go of the grip on the push without losing control of the pole. This also cuts down on hand fatigue since you won't need to have a tight hold on the grip.

3) Trekking poles are not canes, although you can lean on them. Since many only have experience with a walking staff or stick picked up during the hike, you're usually placing the stick in front of you and walking to it. They're more about giving your hand something to do as you stroll through the forest.

Pole tips trailing behind, opposite leg and pole in synch and with same cadence. Allow them to push you forward each step.

However, what trekking poles really do is act like propelling sticks that help to push you along. When used as intended, the grips and your hands will be swinging on a pendulum movement from in front to behind you - the pole tips are nearly always close behind you to farther behind you. Said differently, your pole tips are trailing your body, and on each placement to the ground your arm uses them to give a tiny push. The tricky part is getting the rhythm of your arms and poles to match your steps; its not right pole with right leg like that of a cane, it is right pole with left leg striding. So your right arm synchs to your left leg step and left arm to the right leg step. By having a cadence of opposite arm to opposite leg, your body will be in better balance. This is the ideal. At first it will be like trying to chew gum and walk at the same time, but it will become natural. Find this rhythm and your pace will increase.

If you were to go for a brisk walk (without poles), your arms would pendulum back and forth, synching to the opposite leg. It's how we're wired. For some reason when some put a pole in their hand, there's a predisposition that the pole and leg closer to one another should be in lock step – the robot walk. It's probably because we start thinking too much?

The use of trekking poles can reduce the impact to your knees on those rugged step-downs and those multiple mile down-mountains. When faced with step-downs, place both poles on the step below you and then use your arms to soften the effects of you and your pack weight assaulting your knees.

Trekking poles have a small "basket" called a day basket down near the tip. This is to help prevent them from plummeting deep into mud or between rocks. They come with your trekking poles and should be used. (When using trekking poles in snow, the points will sink into the snow, thereby shortening the pole's length. The pole will need to be lengthened accordingly and day baskets will need to be swapped with bigger diameter snow baskets, which will stop the pole at the snow level.)

Trekking poles not only help your balance on dry land, they also help with fording streams. When fording, always face up stream so you can see if possible debris is headed your way. Always unbuckle your hip belt and sternum strap first, making for an easier exit from the pack if you lose your balance. Packs will become dreadfully heavy when wet, but your first priority is staying safe to hike another day.

Whacking your poles together and yelling "Hey Bear!" has sent almost all of my black bear encounters thundering over hill and dale. One of the times it didn't work was when a momma sow had her three cubs nearby - a tense moment indeed. The other was with a black bear in New Jersey that was a tad too familiar with humans, lingering near me for a little too much time despite my yelling.

Rather than carrying a clothesline, upon reaching camp I'd pound my two poles into the ground about 18 inches apart and hang my sweat soaked hiking shirt on them for a quicker dry.

On my hiking poles I have two Velcro pads stuck to each of the shafts about 18 inches apart. When the poles are spaced out in the ground as just mentioned, those four pads are stuck to the four Velcro corners I sewed onto my "Hiker To Town" bandana (which I lettered with a large Sharpie), creating a roadside billboard. One never wants a willing driver to be confused as to your intentions when burgers, showers, and laundry are just down the road. For emergency repairs, each pole also has two feet of duct tape spooled around them just under the grips.

To improve the odds of finishing your hike with poles you start with, consider when taking a break try to place or lean your poles on a tree or object that is up-trail (the direction you're traveling) since getting going again means you'll walk into them if they slip your mind, which it has for some, and avoids the walk back feeling like a chucklehead.

As you can see, trekking poles have multiple uses beyond that of keeping you upright. I highly recommend them.

No Rain. No Pain. No Gain. No Maine.

Rain! It's as common to an AT thru-hike as cold is to winter.

Before your thru-hike starts, invariably there will be massive rain events at your home neighborhood. Winds of 20 mph with gusts over 40, rain coming down in sheets and the clouds and fog will meld together (never can tell when in the mountains if I'm in clouds or fog). "Nasty" can describe what could be outside your door one not so fine day before you start your hike; another way to think is, "Just another day on the AT. "

Wading into some of that wetness – rain practice - mentally and physically can be part of the preparation. Since going out for a day hike usually coincides with nice weather, having no experience with the bad stuff tends to rattle many a hiker. In the past, that constant roar of high winds used to unnerve me. Somehow I acclimated to it where it's no longer an issue. The one thing I thought I'd never get comfortable with was the distant BoomBoomBoom. Where there's thunder there's lightning and nothing makes me jump out of my shoes higher than a cloud-to-ground CRACK. Don't think I'm alone on that. To be clear, I'm not comfortable with lightning, but rather just a tad less uncomfortable than I used to be.

Rain, on the other hand, is not lightning and really need not be feared. It's annoying and inconvenient, but with the appropriate clothing and pack preparations to keep items dry that must stay dry, walking in rain can be quite manageable.

Over the years I've experimented with my rain gear to help add breathability and weight savings. Out on the PCT, since rain is so rare on that big hike, rain protection isn't as high a priority. On the AT though, rain is infamous. Some years can be downright drenching thanks to jet stream weather patterns. A low rain year on the AT can still far exceed the wettest year on the PCT.

A hiking buddy of mine, Allegheny, thru-hiked the PCT's 2600 miles and had a total of FIVE days of rain. The Appalachian Trail is a whole other beast when it comes to rain. My council to everyone interested in an AT thru-hike is to put a premium on proper, significant rain gear – especially if their start is at the beginning of the northbound season. Cold temps and high elevation rain are a marvelous recipe for hypothermia. I've heard from countless hikers with vast experience in winter camping or rain hiking or high elevation winds, sleet, hail, and snow tell me that the AT almost unhinged them because they never had experienced it all happening at the same time.

My first thru-hike year - what The Weather Channel called the fifth wettest hiking season on record (2004) saw three hurricane remnants move up the trail all the way to Maine. The numerous non-event fords in Maine's 100-Mile Wilderness were transformed into high-drama events as a result of colossal amounts of rain.

How well you manage rain is a significant part of a successful AT thru-hike, so investing in better rain clothing will be money well spent. In the next chapter, "Secret #5: Different Day Same Shirt", I will go into specific considerations regarding foul weather protection.

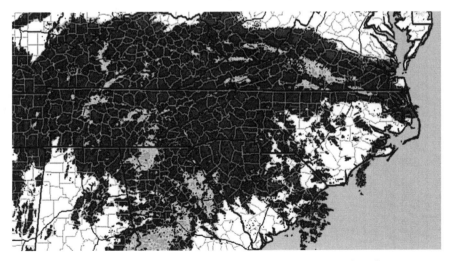

Rain events (dark mass) can be vast and widespread. Hikers must move forward regardless of the wet weather.

A look at any weather event on the AT using Doppler radar can show a scope so large that sitting them out could mean not hiking for days on end. That's not an option in thru-hiking.

Practicing for the inconvenience of rain is difficult. At the very least you can wade out into the next serendipitous howling wind and sideways rain before your hike - consider it rain practice. Of course it's always easier when you know you can return back to the dry house or that tomorrow you won't have to put on that still-wet clothing to make miles again. Some of our preparing can be quite fun and silly.

My take on rain hiking is this: if you protect yourself well, so long as it's not lightning, it really doesn't matter how hard it rains, you'll just walk inside your protective shell. Rain comes in the form of the occasional sprinkle or mist, to the cats-and-dogs deluge that can leave you laughing for being out in such ridiculous weather. Rain walking is sort of a Zen thing – it can be tranquil and texturally different without consequence if you can keep your anxiety at bay, and good rain gear can help you with that. In the absence of lightning, rain is really just a temporary nuisance that affects how you deal with all the wet clothing, crowded shelters or tent set up. The key word here is "temporary"; the sun will shine again. Maybe not tomorrow, but eventually.

I've found that facing rain during a thru-hike has three distinct phases. First, is the Fret Phase (sort of self-explanatory). You realize you can't see the horizon anymore, there's a blurred, bluish fuzziness to an area of the sky and it seems to be getting close. Thoughts like "#!?#!," "Not again" and "Yikes" are fairly common. You throw on your foul weather clothing and pack cover and move on with worry. Second is the Avoidance Phase where it has you dancing, dodging and weaving the puddles as the rain gets heavy, hoping to keep a degree of sock dryness. But if the rain continues hour after hour, despite having wonderful foul weather clothing, rain finds a way to soak you. The third phase comes after failure of the second phase. That's when the Wet Phase completely frees you, liberates you to just go. Gone are the frets of getting wet (you're as wet as a Wahoo off Washington), you know your gear is safe and dry due to your packing strategy, and you're free to just power ahead come hell or deep puddles with nary a thought.

You just embrace the texture. That's when rain is fun. Why I've even just sat down in puddles to eat lunch.

Wearing rain gear is also about staying warm; rain events often bring a dropping temperature and a chilly wind. That is why I don't like ponchos when dealing with these events - they'll flap like a flag on a pole on windy ridge-lines and at higher elevations-that means no windproof warmth. Ponchos are good for hot seasons and humid conditions, but not much for warmth protection and wind chill.

Gearing up for rain.

Preparing your gear for rain need not be troublesome. Some things that need to stay dry need extra attention – sleeping bag, clothes, and food bag. Certainly with today's digital addictions, those devices will need safe-guarding too.

Sleeping bags, whether synthetic or down, usually come with their own stuff sack (down bags) or compression bag (synthetic bags) from the manufacturer. All you need to do to ensure that they always arrive at camp dry is to incorporate the use of a dry bag. Once you have your bag in its own provided sack (stuffing it from the foot end first to let the air out of the hood end), just drop that into one of the ultralight dry bags now on the market. Both REI and Sea To Summit make ultralight dry bags that only weight about two ounces. The dry bag size I recommend is a 20-liter since it will minimize the difficulty of dropping the provided bag inside the dry bag. Once in the dry bag, give it a squeeze to push the air out and then just roll down the dry bag top three times or more, buckle it and then continue to hike without wet fret.

The same ultralight dry bags can be used as a clothes bag so you always have that second outfit dry and toasty to change into. The same Ultra-Sil 20-liter size also makes for a good option as your food bag since we never sleep with our food. It needs to be hung either on bear cables (sometimes provided at shelters) or in a tree when tenting or hammocking out. Thunderstorms rage in at 3 am, and your food can get soaked if not protected in a dry bag.

Older techniques of lining your backpack with a trash bag (contractor grade thickness) help to keep all things inside dry during a wet day. Sea To Summit makes a slightly better fitting version called a Pack Liner in 50, 70 and 90-liter sizes. My thru-hiking pack is 50 liters, so I added one of the 70-liter liners allowing enough space for the top to roll down before buckling.

Using a pack liner does not forgo using a rain cover for your pack. A pack rain cover is still your first line of defense and useful since it keeps your pack dry and prevents it from taking on water weight, which therefore keeps your pack lighter. You don't want to bring a sopping wet pack into your tent at night and have it puddle out and get other things wet. Rain is your biggest nuisance out there, cold rain your biggest adversary.

I always *always* like to have multiple lines of defense to combat it. As the hiker season moves forward on the calendar, more adverse weather patterns will start to emerge.

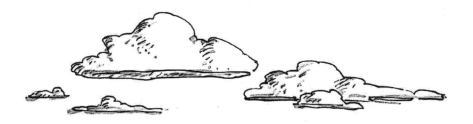

Altocumulus can foretell rain may be a half-day away.

As the land and air heats up with the rising sun, thunderstorms will routinely pop up in late afternoon. On days when I knew these weather events were likely, I'd hike with purpose. I'm all for naps in sunshine on glorious days, sitting on boulders by a stream to have a foot soak in the cool water, but if the forecast called for storms I limited the duration of my breaks. On these days I've often made my 20 mile destination, got my water and was enjoying a hot meal while dry and snug as a bug when the rain drama arrived to put out my campfire. When the cloud-to-ground lightning starts CRACKing, striking the area around your location since you're on a mountain ridgeline, you're glad that there are no chores left to do. You start to feel you're managing the land, weather, and passage at a more savvy level. Not controlling it - managing it. That is how you continue to increase the odds of succeeding in your quest to achieve Thru-hiker status. This also strengthens your emotional side. Moments of good choreography like these elevate your confidence. It's not about luck, it's about you making smart decisions and having them pan out in your favor.

↑ *You are here. Often.*

Secret

Gravity and Counting Ounces.

Having previously backpacked on the heavy side and discovered how to avoid doing so again, I have to say I appreciate the vistas and journey all the more with a lighter load. Joy seems more easily found when the load isn't forcing us to stare down at the dirt and grind it out.

Since gravity literally sucks you down toward the Earth's core while the mountain elevations force you to continue up, you're getting smooshed between the two as they battle. It's hard to know which is the tougher foe, but since gravity influences everything (including your pack weight) it seems to have the edge. The scientific equation of downward force on you and your pack load is:

$G = 32.2 \text{ ft} / S^2$

Gravity (G) sucks, literally. It is the downward force pulling all that we carry towards the center of the Earth. And it wants to do that to every trail gizmo, doodad or dohicky at a speed of 32.2 feet per second squared. It does this every tick of the second hand and it does not discriminate between flat terrain or up-and-down Appalachian Mountain terrain. Only our muscles and damn stubbornness can combat it.

Didn't realize I was going to be talking science, did you? Now let's talk some math.

This Secret is about watching our weight. It matters little whether that weight is in your pack, your pocket, or on your foot; your muscles, resolve and demeanor will have to contend with it. When you're new to backpacking it's easy to overlook what something might weigh – to trivialize an ounce or three. You may hear outrageous stories how some have cut off their toothbrush handles to help avoid a smidgeon of weight from their pack load. You scoff at such things, attribute these actions to knuckle-headery or meds being out of balance. In your life experience you've most likely have never asked the sales person, "Which of these little black dresses weighs less?" or, "Show me you're lightest wingtips, my good man." With that in mind, here's the opening headline:

"Counting ounces isn't fanatical, it's practical."

Now, the story. I had just spent the better part of an hour using my hand-held paper hole-punch on my Crocs. Now before any of you non-hikers report me to the Humane Society, Crocs, as we hikers know, are camp shoes made of closed-cell foam. When they came onto the market years ago, they were a big hit since they weigh so little and offer an alternative to flip-flops.

Flip-flops are a flop with my toes since my little piggies are spaced out like that of a thumb and forefinger. Now before any of you report me to Ripley's Believe It or Not-my feet do look normal by most measures. It's just that flip-flops lose to Crocs in a foot-to-foot competition for trail needs as a camp shoe.

Tops on my list of Crocs advantages is toe protection. I like my toes shielded from harm during those chores around camp – harvesting water, finding firewood, visiting the forest at 2 am to pee while half asleep. And their modest coverage helps when the mosquito season ramps up to its full biting ugliness; a toe is apparently just as delicious as a forehead. Having found at least two-dozen Crocs on the trail, either a left or a right but never a matching left and right, mine go inside rather than outside my pack to dangle, wiggle to-and-fro and find a way to drop with nary a sound. If you'd like to arrive at camp that night with everything you started the morning with, things need to be strapped down securely or put inside the pack.

We long-distance hikers may have gone over the edge when it comes to finding new ways to not carry ounces, so even foamy Crocs get our attention. Mine are a size 11 and weigh in at 6.35 ounces each. For those who have misplaced their calculators since high school algebra, that's 12.7 ounces for the pair. Crocs fresh from the factory have 13 unlucky holes on the top; a few slots on the sides and lots of solid foam make up the remaining 95%. By taking an ordinary paper hole puncher, one may easily punch a 14th or 15th or even a 16th hole. Of course where there's a way to lighten one's load easily, there's a will to get punchy. My right Croc now sports 219 holes, and the left has 221. What do 440 holes of air rather than foam give you other than well-ventilated, stylish slippers? Crocs that now weigh in at 11.7 ounces – a savings of 1 ounce.

So, for every 16 steps taken, an entire pound will not be carried. Interesting, isn't it? Let's continue the math, factoring in once again that 2000 steps a mile is not uncommon - 1 ounce saved per step equals 1 pound saved every 16 steps. That results in 125 pounds not carried every mile. So that means on a 10-mile hike I avoid carrying 1,250 pounds.

Still with me? The crazy part - the almost unbelievable part - is that by saving one inconsequential ounce from my Croc camp shoes and then going on a 2,185 mile AT thru-hike means not carrying a consequential 273,125 pounds. It's relevant to restate, "Counting ounces isn't fanatical, it's practical."

Weight, per se, will never determine whether you'll achieve Thru-hiker status, but it will have a huge impact on your emotional strength. I've known hikers who carried 60 lbs and made it and others who carried 20 that didn't. But I don't think it's going too far out on a limb to say we would all have a wider smile at the top of a mountain vista carrying 25 lbs rather than 45 lbs. We most likely got there sooner with a better pace and without our spirit getting so beaten up. Let's continue this discovery of weight that our body, legs and willpower must schlep.

Out of common sense and a desire to address the burden of weight from gravity, years ago I changed out my impressive, stainless steel Leatherman Wave - at 9 ounces - for the tiny, keychain pocket knife by Swiss Army, which weighs a mere 1 ounce.

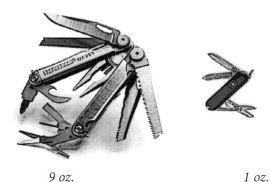

9 oz.   *1 oz.*

The Wave is part multi-tool, part Transformer; it put the "Swiss Army Knife" concept on steroids and made Leatherman famous. Certainly The Wave would be more capable of helping me build a yacht to get off a desert island or conquer 300 Spartans. That first time I went backpacking with my backpack somehow tipping the scale at 54 lbs, a Leatherman Wave was in its pocket. Surely going out for six months of wilderness adventure requires either that or a Crocodile Dundee bowie knife? However, an AT Thru-hike isn't about survival; it's about the journey, simplicity, and freedom. You won't be entering into hand-to-hand combat with Yogi and Booboo. That would be a clear misconception.

In its defense, the keychain knife has scissors, nail file, even a toothpick that was very useful during my thru-hikes. It's itty-bitty tweezers, which I found feeble, never got used, but the nail file proved valuable at getting the sock fuzz out of the nooks and crannies of my big toes.

The Wave, however, had a saw in case I had the urge to fell a few trees and build a log cabin. It had pliers for pulling out a thorn out of the wounded paw of a sore foot lion or tent stake from the ground – quite practical. It also had a Phillips-head screwdriver just in case the car driving me into town broke down and needed repairs, and it sported a can opener for opening all those cans of Spam and Dinty Moore beef stew in my food bag, … or not. Boldly, I chose to lose some capability to save the half-pound (8 ounces).

Before we move further ahead, you need to understand the journey I've been on. I have a confession, not that I've sinned, but that I once mocked, yes, mocked those who cut off toothbrush handles to save a smidgen of weight. I once believed that if I spared no expense and bought every wilderness conquering doodad that the odds of my adventure's success would increase. Because I was too arrogant to think I could learn a new trick or two from others, I'd scoff at toothbrush handles being shortened, and discounted a shaved ounce here or there as lame-brained, delusional idiocy. Now, knowing the effects of gravity, humbled by the difficulty of the AT's relentless ascents against that formidable foe, my transition to removing a mere ounce out of Crocs and being braggadocious in doing so is a fair distance to travel. Once one knows about gravity and its effect on our legs, mindset, and emotional resolve, it's shortsighted not to watch our weight.

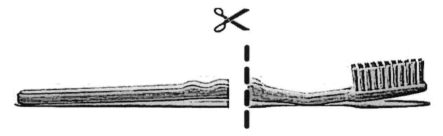

Your handle may be a "luxury" item you'll want, otherwise cut that sucker off and avoid another quarter of a million pounds.

Once I discovered that watching our weight (with our gear, that is) had its benefits for our legs and stamina, I willingly changed out to the Swiss Army Knife keychain model. Its scissors (to open my camp dinners) and tooth-pick and nail file were the only items I ever needed. Love that toothpick.

By swapping the "Transformer multi-tool" for the puny keychain knife, I avoided a half-pound every time I lifted my left leg and every time I lifted my right leg. Wonderful things started to happen. Revisiting our 2000-steps-per-mile model, I avoided carrying 1000 pounds on a 1-mile hike. In a 15-mile day with its 30,000 steps, I didn't have to carry 15,000 pounds!

Virginia is the state with a thru-hike's greatest number of miles. At 550.3 miles (at the time of this writing), hikers contract what is known as "The Virginia Blues," an emotional malaise that can be their demise. Those 550 Virginia miles translate into 1,100,600 steps where each leg is lifted, placed and lifted again. Saving those 8 small ounces avoids an enormous 550,300 pounds carried through Virginia alone. All of a sudden mileage becomes easier; never easy - just easier.

On a Georgia to Maine thru-hike, simply because I changed my knife, I avoided carrying 2,500,000 lbs. Anyone think they might have better odds of achieving a thru-hike if they weren't carrying two and a half million pounds? Let's wed that to the weight saved on my Crocs and we've avoided just fewer than three million pounds. Can I get a hallelujah?

Sometimes weight is hidden in plain sight, such as our stuff sacks. *Not what is in our stuff sacks, but the stuff sacks themselves.* With a mindset to have everything we need but with an eye towards lightening our burden to legs and spirit, I discovered that changing out five of my "durable," heavier stuff sacks for five of the ultra-light ripstop nylon ones, one full pound dropped out of my load – another FIVE MILLION POUNDS avoided from Georgia to Maine just by swapping out stuff sacks. Crazy, right?

The purchasing rational is easy to understand: you're going on an epic adventure and your organizational stuff sacks must be robust and strong. But we're not battling dragons or swinging them like nunchucks onto the heads of trolls. Our stuff sacks will be inside another protective shell – our backpack – so switching to the ultra-light versions is not cutting corners on performance, just cutting corners on dead weight.

"I love carrying a heavy backpack."

~ No one, ever.

"Ugg!"   *"Ahh."*

Save a total of 10 pounds (40 lb pack down to 30) and in an end-to-end thru-hike you avoid 50,000,000 pounds of smile- erasing burden.

Save big.

The journey of discovery in watching our weight starts with The Big Three – Backpack, Shelter and Sleeping Bag. But it all adds up or subtracts down, as the three items discussed previously (Crocs, knife and stuff sacks) highlight how easily 8 million pounds can be avoided.

Fanaticism in avoiding weight can get misguided, though, in my opinion. Some will focus so much on the numbers that things they'll need for a joyful journey will be omitted, leaving them vulnerable to failure. When weight is the only consideration without any thought to the livability of those choices – such as tents that are hard to get in and out of in bad conditions - difficulty is added to the adventure. (We'll dive more into this dynamic in the gear section.) It is important to remember that thru-hiking requires you to be fully self-sufficient – have everything you'll need with you at all times. This will give you options in the face of adversity.

One rainy day on the trail, I met a hiker who arrived late to an overly full shelter. After proudly boasting about his ultra-light pack weight, he carried no form of shelter, not even a tarp. With literally no place for him on the floor to sleep, he had to sit up on the front edge to sleep that night. His indignation and sour words written in the register were ridiculous. You carry no shelter and take it out on others when you don't get your ideal scenario to play out. I felt no sympathy for him, especially after he bragged about how light his load was.

It is always better to have what you need, regardless of weight, and not use it rather than to need it and not have it. Never mind the cliché, but these sayings become colloquial in our language because they touch on an emotional truth. (FYI – I slept great that night, albeit like a sardine between others.)

We like options in a 2000-mile adventure. It can be rationalized that certain items are not needed when thinking of the "ideal" scenario. It is wiser to plan for facing adversity, having what may be needed rather than planning on everything going to plan without consequence. Celebrate the ideal, but have options when adversity comes knocking at your tent door.

"Have everything you need and a few things you want."

Having everything you need and a few things you want means you should try to limit your luxury items. Before the hike starts you may not know which things you truly want. As the hike moves forward you start to understand, for you personally, what is essential and what is superfluous. I couldn't be Postcard without my art supplies, a full pound consisting of a drawing pad and artisan ink markers in a Ziploc. If you have a bad back, maybe you want a full-length sleeping pad that's 3 inches thick?

"If you don't use it everyday, maybe you shouldn't be carrying it?"

~ Thru-hiker trail wisdom

This trail wisdom has its merit, but there are some exceptions.

Even though the AT has some 250 shelters or lean-tos, having your own form of shelter in the event that injury prevents your arrival to these structures or the conditions at the shelter may have you choose elsewhere – a Towner's drunken bonfire party (seen it), large snake in the rafters (seen that, too), etc – it's nice to have the option to move on. A First Aid Kit hopefully doesn't ever get used, but it seems wise to have one.

This wisdom is focused on weight management and minimizing the drama that can find you on a thru-hike. As the journey moves forward, and with it your comprehension of what you need versus what you want, stuff gets mailed home. It's quite likely you'll be reducing your pack weight as assessments and adjustments are made along the way. It's been reported that at Neels Gap, the Mountain Crossings outfitter there in an old stone building known as the Walasi-Yi Center, they box up and mail out four tons of gear each new thru-hike season. And that is only 30 miles into the journey! It has also been reported that 30% of the dreamers decide to "Come off the trail" there too.

Whatever the decisions are that got you to the trail, if they aren't making the journey easier, lighter, more effortless, then zag. This is a volunteer endeavor; it should bring a smile to your face. Remaining flexible, assessing and adjusting doesn't make you less of a person, it makes you a savvy hiker who's thru-hiking with the hopes of becoming a Thru-hiker.

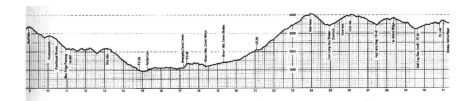

Gravity doesn't care whether you're walking on flat terrain or the countless ups and downs of the Appalachian Trail.

Lightening your load will widen your smile, but never do so if it means being unprepared.

Secret

Different day. Same shirt.

Your protection on a thru-hike is not a big honkin' Crocodile Dundee bowie knife or Elmer Fudd double barrel; those are useless against cold mountain temps and torrential rain events. Your protection is your clothing, so it is important to choose wisely. With that in mind, cotton, although the advertising claims it is the fabric of life, is also the enemy of the outdoors. When worn, when sweated into, when wet from rain, many bad things happen. Wet cotton will make you colder – not good. It stays wet for long periods, not remotely drying and thus becoming heavy – also not good.

It also becomes abrasive when damp with perspiration leading to chaffing – just plain bad. In my opinion, you should only take one item of cotton on your thru-hike: a bandana. Performance fabrics – polyester or other synthetics – are designed to wick (pull sweat away to dry quickly) – good. Synthetic fabrics can add a level of warmth even when wet – also good. Most have a stretch quality that stay true to shape and are quite thin and lightweight, reducing the odds of chaffing – very good. Their one downside is they can absorb your body odor – manageable. Since you'll be on a full-blown wilderness adventure, your clothing will be of all performance fabrics.

In suburbia, we choose our clothes for vanity. Come on, admit it. Seldom do we put on a garment to make ourselves look hideous before we walk out the front door to take on the world. Vanity in clothing is not a bad thing. Look good, feel good. Feel good, and confidence enters the room with you for all to see – never a bad strategy in business.

Vanity in your hiking attire is no different. Look good, feel good. Feel good, step good. Step good and you make good miles without falling (hopefully). I always encourage everyone to choose a hiking outfit that makes them feel handsome or pretty. After the laughing stops, I explain why every photo taken during the daytime should be with this outfit on.

Here's is your thru-hiking clothes secret: Just two outfits.

A) One complete outfit you can hike in every day.

B) One complete camp outfit to get dry and warm if needed.

C) Full foul-weather protection – rain jacket and pants.

D) Not only less clothing, but clothing that weighs less.

The only way to avoid carrying your entire closet and excessive weight is to have a hiking wardrobe that creates options. A thru-hiker will have two complete outfits of appropriate fabrics for the traditional time period of a thru-hike, which can also be described as a three-season wardrobe. These items will allow you many options of layering to contend with the varied weather. This omits a winter start, which would mean winter weight, mountaineering style attire. The southern Appalachians in March can still (likely) have snow events at elevation, but they are temporary. This is not as much an issue with an April start, but each season is different and thru-hikers must adapt to the seasonal trends.

Here is a list of clothing you will need:

- *1 Hiking outfit you wear every day – Pant, top, brief*
- *1 Camp outfit to get dry and warm – Pant, top, brief (for sleep)*
- *2 Pairs of hiking socks*
- *2 Pairs of sock liners*
- *2 Insulated jackets – One synthetic & one down or a second synthetic if allergic to down (One coat during warmer months)*
- *2 Lightweight hats – One wide brim (optional), one fleece*
- *2 Lightweight gloves – One during warmer months*
- *1 Rain jacket & rain pant*
- *Camp shoes (I like Crocs)*
- *Bandana (I like mine on my front shoulder strap for sweat. The only cotton you'll have.)*

Optional Extras (Luxury items):

- *Wind Shirt, like a Patagonia Houdini*
- *Gaiters, if you don't wear pants*
- *Insulated vest, most likely synthetic*
- *Base layers (Midweight long underwear top & bottom), maybe two depending on your start date or if there's a lingering winter. Your own sensitivity to cold and*

metabolism will determine these. Do you get cold in July or are you a furnace in January?

At first blush when one hears just two outfits, it sounds like a meager amount of clothing. But when you list it out as I just have, it is a collection of items that can be used in multiple combinations, even used together by doubling. Much depends on that year's weather trends, your start date, your hike direction, and your metabolism (whether you get cold easily or not). Either way, adjustments can be made during the journey.

The first months of a thru-hike are teetering between mild spring temps, lingering cold winter temps and warm, sunny days. The reality is the Appalachian Trail will most likely give you the texture of all of them. Wild temperature swings are common from weather events moving from west to east. Additionally I've had hail, sleet, snow, ice, thunderstorms, lightning, gale force winds, flooding, (some of those at the same time) and hurricane remnants. Preparing for this variety can be instrumental in keeping your emotional strength dialed up. Being cold and wet can test the resolve of the stoutest hiker. My clothes list was created to combat this texture one faces; thru-hiking requires having options.

There will be scenarios where your hiking shirt and your rain jacket will be inadequate to keep you warm, even with your pack cinched to your back. Since carrying a backpack up and down the AT will have you drenched in sweat, a chill wind can quickly gang up on you, bringing hypothermia into the picture. In the past I'd only carry my camp jacket, usually one of down insulation, but then I'd run into sideways rain and 40 degree temperatures on a Smokys ridgeline without an insulation layer that could stand up to wetness. Since I knew that a down coat must stay dry to work its magic, I found myself starting to shiver – an early sign of hypothermia. Fortunately this played out just as the trail reached the public road at Newfound Gap in the Smokys, and I was able to hitch a ride from a generous driver. Once in his truck and heading down to Gatlinburg, I asked if he could crank up the heater to help stop the shivering that my mental power couldn't control.

This type of scenario is not uncommon and, as a result, I recommend that each thru-hiker have two forms of insulation – a synthetic insulation that will deliver warmth even when wet, and a warmer down one for camp. The style of jacket for moving and making your miles and that can also tolerate your sweat or rain are the newer synthetic jackets like a Patagonia Nano Puff or Nano Air, REI Revelcloud, The North Face Thermoball, or Arc'teryx Atom, to name a few. They all have 60 grams of a synthetic insulation under various proprietary names such as Primaloft or Coreloft.

This type of garment gives you a hiking day warmth option that can be worn on top of your hiking shirt on a cold dry day or worn underneath your rain jacket on cold wet days. Synthetic tops also have minimal weight and bulk, unlike the volume associated with most fleece tops. Some info says these synthetic insulated tops can still deliver 80% of their warmth even when wet, making them ideal for the high-sweating activity of backpacking. The synthetic top gives you hiking day warmth options early and late in the thru-hiker season where the elevation and/or latitude on the hemisphere can add temperature drama. During the warmer months you will choose to carry either it or your down jacket, which I'll address in your second outfit.

Newer, warmer jackets of synthetic and water repellant down blends are now available in some models. These new hybrid blends of Primaloft Silver can retain a full 90% of their warmth when wet while still knocking down a 60 mph wind. These jackets, such as REI Stratocloud, are new to the hiking landscape and will be prized when more of you discover them.

Sock liners will also be quite valuable to the hiker (or should I say the hiker's feet) due to the high-mileage foot sweating and the numerous rainy days. In each case, the soft fluffy nap of hiker socks becomes compressed and matted, and the soft fluffy fabric becomes a coarse, abrasive fabric that rubs against your foot skin with every step. Wearing a sock liner acts as a buffering layer that can reduce the odds of friction and blisters. Sock liners are thin, snug socks that stay close to your foot, sort of like hose for your feet. I recommend them since the AT has lots of rain and 90% humidity days. They also serve as a good sleeping sock at night.

Hiking sock material and style will vary from hiker to hiker. Wool or synthetic fibers are a must. No cotton anything. Smartwool, REI, and Darn Tough are excellent choices. But this will be covered further in the Happy Hiker Feet section.

A synthetic under short or brief is more an optional choice than a requirement. I liked wearing the close fitting Nike Pro performance brief that looks a bit like cycling shorts. They offer some modesty to crowded shelter clothes changes, but even they have to be changed out to your other pair at times when you are really cold and wet. Originally I used to carry one brief, but at 3 ounces, the second brief is a nice luxury item that can get you warm and dry faster in some cases. Often, though, just getting out of the big items (pants, top and socks) gets you warm quickly with or without any brief on at all.

Sometimes going behind the shelter to change clothes is impractical due to rain. I have at times announced to a full shelter to look the other way for the next minute since I had to take everything off to get into my dry, warm second outfit. Since all thru-hikers go through this, it's pretty common. Funny announcements like, "Ladies, please look the other way, I don't want to ruin it for your boyfriend or husband," are great fun for what can be a short but awkward strip-down in front of complete strangers looking the other way. Just more of the texture that is an AT adventure.

The close-fitting performance brief I wear can help reduce the one painful issue besides blisters that hikers face early on – chafing up high between the legs.

Carrying Body Glide for chafing is essential early in your hike before you lose some of that cityness body flubber. Body Glide quickly reduces the pain caused by inflamed skin due to the friction of making miles. Chafing will bring your day to an abrupt halt. With it applied, I've been able to continue to make my destination without issue. I then apply it again in camp, which speeds recovery for a chafe-free tomorrow.

Chafing is a common problem early in most hikes, and it's certainly not limited to just the upper, inner thighs. Your buns (buttocks cheeks) can also experience the irritation as well as nipples or armpits. So what is Body Glide? It is an anti-friction balm that resembles a deodorant stick. Until you become a more svelte version of yourself, you should carry it. Wonderfully, it also helps to prevent that other nasty issue of hot-spots on feet that become blisters. Since a hot-spot is actually a high friction location, you can also rub it on your feet to reduce the odds of a hot-spot becoming a full-blown blister.

Body Glide, an anti-friction stick, and Bag Balm are
two additions I used throughout my journeys.

A short story on Body Glide: I had been traveling with another hiker named Masterplan for a week or two. We both had an attacking demeanor to mileage and a friendly nature. On Day 2 in the Smokys, the weather was waffling between fog and light rain, giving us an opportunity to pass over the highest point on the AT, Clingmans Dome, as long as we could complete the 25 mile distance to the next shelter. (Every one wants to be in a shelter on a rainy night.) My issue that hiking day was I had ran out of Body Glide the previous day and, still having more than my fair share of cityness flubber, I was chafing terribly between my upper, inner thighs. Although I enjoyed Masterplan's fellowship, I informed him at a shelter just before Clingmans Dome, at 16 miles, my chafing pain was so bad I'd start bleeding if I took another step. Masterplan graciously offered me his Body Glide despite knowing where I was about to rub it; a grander gesture would be hard to find. So I went behind the shelter, applied the Body Glide to my crotch, upper thighs and buttocks cheeks. When I handed it back to him, naturally he said, "Umm ...Keep it." "Ahh, yea. Of course," I said. We packed up and to my amazement did another 9 miles, crossing over Clingmans Dome and all the way to the next shelter, free of pain.

Bag Balm is a thick, lanolin suave that when applied to your feet at the end of each hiking day, will keep your feet soft and new by morning. Before my first thru-hike, I once witnessed a hiker arrive at the shelter, take off his socks, massage this suave into them, slip on his sock liners and then go about his chores. Since I knew very little about making miles and backpacking at this time, and the fact that we all learn from each other, I watched him intently, especially since I noticed he had three 2000-Miler patches on his backpack. That's how I discovered Bag Balm and came to use it on my feet during my hikes. Good stuff, and it can be bought in a small 1 ounce tin. It took two for a Georgia-to-Maine journey. Bag Balm is a Vermont standard, primarily used on the dairy cows to cut down on irritation to their udders.

Returning to our wardrobe, having two glove liners and possibly two lightweight fleece hats in addition to two jacket options allow you to wear one during the hiking day and still have a dry one once in camp. Having two allows you to put them on top of one another for added warmth, or to put the wet one on top of the dry one to speed the dry time. Glove liners provide warmth and good dexterity when using trekking poles or for all your duties around camp – harvesting water, operating your stove, eating, or drawing postcards. My favorite glove is Mountain Hardwear's Power Stretch, but there are plenty of other close-fitting stretchy ones, just see what suits you.

What's nice about a fleece hat is how when the inside is soaked from sweat, you can reverse it (turn it inside out), putting the dry outside next to your head and letting the wet inside evaporate. This reversing option is like having two hats for the weight of one! This is called "working" your clothes. (There'll be times when you'll work your socks or a wet tent on the outside of your pack during the hiking day if they are soaked.) Since you'll be wearing this hat around camp in front of others in the early and late months of the trek, make sure you select one with vanity. There's no harm in having a good looking hat that matches your jackets. Just be sure to choose one that's as light as a Frito.

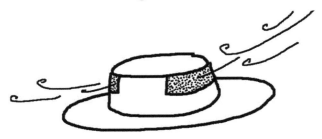

The Outdoor Research (OR) Transit Sun Hat and the Columbia Bora Bora Booney II are wide brim hats that have won my favor as of late. All my wide brim hats have one specific feature: vented fabric around the dome. Carrying a backpack in the mountains of the AT means to sweat like a waterfall, so having vents let heat escape and permits the occasional breeze to find your hot head.

I also like a wide brim hat for the different times of the season. Early in spring, the trees have no foliage so many hikers spend their time hiking with sunburned foreheads. By the time you reach the Mid-Atlantic states, there are hot temps through treeless farmland, so the wide brim can offer a touch of cooling shade.

At times when the ideal hat didn't present itself, I'd seek out one that had a mesh inner liner in the dome then cut precise, inch-round vent holes around the circumference in the solid outside fabric. The mesh inner layer keeps the bugs from getting in to bite my sweet skin. Yes, I'll MacGyver anything if it adds to performance; only I'll try to do it with a nod to making it look good too. Items that look good while being good in performance is just an added benefit.

The result of looking good as you arrive in camp will have everyone thinking what a smart, savvy looking thru-hiker you are, even if you just walked into a tree a hundred feet back. When you have this, that, and other thing flopping around on the outside of your pack, looking like a mix between a one-man-band and a Rube Goldberg contraption, you look a bit like you're trying to figure it out rather than being James Bond of the wilderness. Of course none of these stylistic differences has an effect on whether you make it or not, I just always challenge the people I help to get all their gear inside their packs. If it dangles, it can fall and land with a whisper on the trail and be lost forever. I've lost only one thing in 5000 miles...my wide brim hat was left in the back of a pickup after a hitchhike to town. That was a really nice hat too. But the number of items I've found on the trail that fell from a pack without the hiker knowing is in the hundreds. You'd think that a 2 pound, full leather hiking boot would make quite a "thud", but hikers constantly lose things that are flopping around on packs if not securely lashed down.

Now that some of the smaller items are covered, let's talk the big things – pants. In recent years, pants have seen an increase in what I really love: stretch fabrics. If you've always opted for the classic convertible hiking pant of lightweight nylon or polyester fabrics, they're still valid, but the newer stretch hiking pants are just wonderful feeling. They offer better freedom of movement for some of the AT hiking that looks nothing like a prototypical smooth footpath. Even when the trail is civilized, stretch fabric pants have an ease of movement that deserves your consideration. Most of these stretch pants also offer a degree of water and wind resistance. Their water resistance sheds the early morning dew that clings to the trail foliage and when wearing waterproof footwear, dry socks will find you more often. A light shower will roll off these stretchy fabrics rather than be absorbed like many other materials. During the early and late months, their wind resistance (some knock down 25 mph winds) can help add warmth on those higher elevation ridgelines. Also known as "soft shell" stretch fabrics, they breathe, shed light water, reduce the effects of wind, and act as a gaiter to help keep footwear debris free and socks a bit dryer. Their one downside is that during the warmer months they block summer breezes through the Mid Atlantic lower elevations.

On both my thru's, I wore long pants for a number of reasons. As mentioned above, they help with warmth early and late in the season. By covering your legs you'll have fewer nicks and scrapes and bleeding from trail foliage and rocks. Although the AT is well maintained, rigid twigs on bushes lining the trail will scratch the heck out of you. Additionally, long pants keep the biting insects (mosquitos, deer flies and black flies) off your legs when you're in camp and not moving constantly. But be warned, some of those little bastards will bite you right through your clothes (especially those pesky deer flies).

I wore convertible pants on my first hike and learned that zipping off the legs doesn't have to be an all-or-nothing proposition. I found by just unzipping the knee, but not removing the lower half, my legs were protected while still letting in the breezes. If they don't have a built-in belt, I found that one of the Bison nylon belts that have an infinite adjustment buckle worked well. Rather than traditional holes for tightening, it uses a clamp that can be moved in any increment – I call it an infinity buckle. You're going to lose a bunch of weight, so that kind of adjustment buckle helps. You'll probably even get your teenage waistline back.

Pants are not the only way though. Shorts are fairly obvious, aren't they? Some kilts will also show up from time to time. Despite colder temps, many will be seen in shorts since when hiking, the human motor is an excellent heater. But stopping in those high mountain chills with sweat-soaked clothes means cold will find you quick unless a patch of sun can be found. I constantly meet those who claim they're not as sensitive to cold and those who are very sensitive. Everyone is different so your outfit needs to address it. Another choice I make is to have one of my hiking tops and pants in black. Black absorbs heat from the sun where light colors reflect it. If

I wasn't "Postcard" I could be "Cupcake" - getting cold is easy for me and having some black helps turn the most meager amount of sun to extra warmth.

Some pants that I like are the REI Screeline, Mistral or Stretch Endeavor, North Face Nimble, Mountain Hardwear Chockstone, Prana Stretch Zion, Arc'teryx Gamma LT or Perimeter, Patagonia Simple Guide and the Mammut Sultana Pants to highlights a few men's stretchy, water and wind resistant pants. Women's versions of many of these pants are also available. (Model names, despite success, invariably get changed or dropped, so be flexible if not found.)

One other detail is my choice of size for my camp jacket. Knowing how much weight you will lose and with it your size, where I'd normally wear a men's large, my thru-hike camp jacket was a men's medium. Although snug early in the hike, it will become ideal very soon. The tighter fit will keep you warmer in camp when that human heater/motor isn't cranked up by making miles. The one-size-smaller approach will keep you warmer up north when there's less of you to fill up your normal size coat. And a smaller size means less weight and volume in the pack. Warmer, lighter, smaller, just by changing the size – brilliant.

Your hiking shirt can follow two paths. Having two means one can be long sleeve for cool days and one can be short sleeve for sunny and warm days. Or in my case, since I get cold easily, two long sleeves were my choice. However long the sleeve, the one you wear during the hike will benefit you if the fabric wicks. These performance fabrics dry very fast and keep you warm when wet. Hiking shirts have crew necks (the low T-Shirt-like collars) or the mid-high, mock necks that have a quarter-length zipper down to your chest. I prefer these zip mock necks since you can easily zip down to cool down or zip up to warm up.

In March and April, the weather on the AT can be sunny and warm one day and snowy the next. A base layer top of the mid-weight variety can be used as your second "camp" shirt or as an additional third shirt if lingering winter trends persist. Carrying the bottoms would also be a consideration. If weather patterns change, you can always mail it home.

Remember my top-line proclamation: clothing is your protection, and the main reason hikers "come off the trail" is due to emotional distress. Staying warm is as strategic as it is common sense. Besides, some of these second items mean a minimal weight impact and a maximum impact on your emotional well-being. But we'll get to the specific weight of these items later in this section.

Let's now discuss your second outfit for camp: One camp outfit you change into and wear on days when the hiking outfit is cold and wet – Pant, top, sock liner, hiking sock, down insulation jacket, fleece hat, glove liner, camp shoe.

Sweaty hiker clothes drying on the anti-mouse food hangers.

In discussing your hiking outfit we've touched on a number of points that crossover to your camp outfit. Case in point: your camp jacket being down (if you're not allergic) rather than synthetic. Where synthetic insulation has certain performance advantages, the choices cited earlier are not as thick or as warm as a down coat. With that in mind, your camp jacket needs to be warmer mainly because you'll no longer have that human heater cranked up from making miles. Cold will find us more easily around camp as we rest up. We're also no longer wearing our backpacks that cover about a third of our core. At sunset - known as Hikers' Midnight - the cold air sinks to the gaps and valleys. Warmer clothing such as that down jacket becomes more strategic here. Add a hot meal for dinner and maybe some hot chocolate afterwards (my habit) to generate extra warmth, and you'll be all toasty inside and out.

Down is the lightest and most compressible insulation with a better warmth-to-weight ratio than synthetic. Using either duck or goose feathers, it is only vulnerable to wetness, hence we don't want to sweat into it or use it under our rain gear. Best to just keep it safe and dry in your pack until camp. Now, if you're allergic to down, then just add a second synthetic insulated top and use both together if needed.

When selecting down coats, you'll see numbers like 650-, 700-, 800- or even 850-fill power down. It may seem like an 800-fill down is warmer than a 650, but this is a common misconception and is not true. These numbers connote the quality of the feather used. One ounce of *800*-fill power goose *down* will loft to *800* cubic inches. The larger the *down* cluster, the more mature the *bird* from which it came. Fewer down clusters are required to fill the garment so they tend to be lighter in weight and compress to a smaller size as a result. There are fewer 800 rated feathers on a bird (usually from the breast and underside), making these jackets more expensive. They also have less quill than say a 550 down and won't work their way through the shell fabric as easily. However, each fill power can keep you warm while managing weight well.

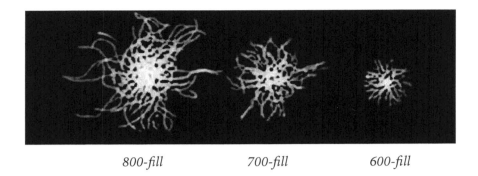

800-fill   *700-fill*   *600-fill*

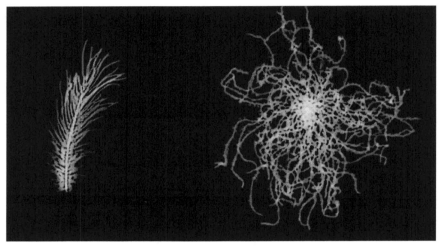

Lower quality Pin-feather   *High quality down cluster*

550-fill   *850-fill*

Duck down tends to look less poofy when lofted up due to having more oils on the feathers than goose. Whenever one washes down, never, ever use normal household detergent since it's designed to remove our human oils from the textiles. This will also remove the oils on the down feathers that help them loft up when our 98.6 degree body heat gets close to them. Less loft means less warmth. Washing of down garments should be done with specific agents like Nikwax Down Wash, which is a water-based cleaner, or similar products. Dry using delicate heat with a tennis ball (clean preferably) tossed in to de-clump the feathers. Front loading washers are required; never use a top loader with the center agitator. It can rip the baffles that are holding the feathers in compartments to provide even heat throughout the item. Ripped baffles means migrating feathers and cold spots. Not good.

In really cold situations a hiker can always use both their jackets together. Using the down one closer to your body will help it work better. The closer your 98.6 body temperature is to the down, the warmer and loftier it gets. It's common for hikers who have down sleeping bags that are old or not rated for the conditions being faced to put on more clothing to supplement the bag's warmth. Unfortunately, when they use their rain gear in that strategy, the rain gear blocks their 98.6 from permeating into their sleeping bag's down, preventing it from lofting up and working more efficiently. Rain gear is infamous in its inability to breathe well, so it limits your body heat from reaching the down.

For more than a decade, the outdoor industry has been reinventing itself with a lightweight revolution. Nothing has escaped its attention, so down jackets - like everything else - have been getting lighter and smaller. Using higher lofting, premium 800 fill down, jackets weigh a trifle of their predecessors and compress to the size of a grapefruit. Options to consider are the Marmot Zeus, Patagonia Down Sweater, Mountain Hardwear Ghost

Whisperer, Arc'teryx Thorium, L.L.Bean Ultralight 850 and REI Co-op down jackets. Most include a Durable Water Repellant (DWR) exterior finish on the fabrics, so light rain can be shed. They're not waterproof, just resistant to a small degree.

"Not only do we carry less clothing in a thru-hike, we carry clothing that weighs less."

Please keep this in mind as you assemble your wardrobe: the weight of clothes adds up as well. But that being said, there is one category of apparel where I feel its performance should govern your decision more than just its weight alone: rain gear.

Weathering The ~~Storm~~ Storms.

In everyone's thru-hike a little rain must fall. Heck, a lot of rain will fall. The AT and rain are as natural to one another as peanut butter is to jelly. And why not quote that old Norwegian proverb, "There's no such thing as bad weather, only inappropriate clothing."

Said another way, it's going to rain on your head. Rain on your stuff. Rain in Georgia. Rain in North Carolina and Tennessee. Rain in every state you'll thru-hike. It will lightly mist. It will sprinkle, spritz, and spit on you. Oh yes, it will dump buckets of water on you and your adventure. There'll be cats-and-dogs deluges so heavy that hippos, water buffalo, and elephants will join in. Cross my heart, it will rain so blooming hard you'll swear there are fish in the ocean drier than you.

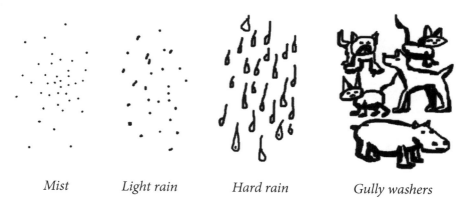

Mist   *Light rain*   *Hard rain*   *Gully washers*

But fret not. There will also be abundant sunshine and bright blue sky. Puffy clouds looking like Popeye or horses or ice cream cones will float by on gentle breezes. Birdsong and fluttering leaves will serenade, moments of perfection will greet you regularly and the dry sock days will outnumber the wet ones.

With good foul weather gear you'll hike your miles, make your destination and keep yourself protected. With the right precautions taken inside your pack as well, you will hike the day in constant rain without a worry. Short of lightning, you'll hike your day feeling a bit invincible. So let's discuss how rain gear will help with that feeling.

Rain fabric – why some wet out and others don't.

Is all rain gear the same? Nope. There, solved that mystery. Hikers are constantly whining about their rain gear wetting out (sticking to them because the water is penetrating the fabric rather than repelling it.) Here's the news flash: no rain gear is really "waterproof," it is however resistant or very resistant to letting rain in for a period of time. How long a period of time can be determined by how highfalutin your gear is.

When you buy rain gear you are actually buying fabric. Waterproof fabric has a different performance from fabric to fabric. Although there are two acknowledged lab tests - one for waterproofness and one for breathability - the clothing industry doesn't routinely publish these performance numbers, which would allow us to make apples to apples comparisons (drats). Unlike in sleeping bags where the EN Rating (European Norm) is widely used to give us truthful temperature ratings, only a few makers of foul weather gear publish their fabric numbers.

Ignorant to the concept that one fabric could be superior to another, I used a Marmot PreCip jacket and pants of a similar performance on my first hike. Many times during rain events the water came through the fabric, but other times it didn't. Sort of perplexing. What I didn't know then that I know now is that rain fabrics have different weather worthiness because they have different weaves, membrane laminations, and coatings that can determine the PSI (pounds per square inch) the fabric can handle. A Precip and other $100 rain jackets have fabrics of 3 to 5 pounds per square inch. These are low performance numbers. It means that some hard hitting, wind driven raindrops can penetrate the fabric. We sometimes think the jacket is wetting out (losing its waterproofness) due to age or quality, but really the weather events are simply exceeding the fabric's performance. That's why the jacket was fine one day but wetted out the next. This is not much of an issue when walking to the mall from your car in civilized polite rain. While the AT has polite rain, it also has rude, pushy, annoying gully washers.

On higher-end fabrics (and therefore higher-priced ones) like Gore-Tex and eVent, you see PSI's in the neighborhood of 40. This almost assuredly means the rain, short of being accompanied by hurricane force winds, isn't coming through as easily. The price of that protection in clothing doubles, triples and in some cases quintuples, but for double the price one can get eight times the weather worthiness. A good trade up, so I quote that cliché: "You get what you pay for."

Since cold rain or the poor management of it can be the undoing of many a thru-hiker's emotional strength,

I put a premium on it. By looking at their labels, you might get lucky to find these numbers, but most likely they'll be hidden. Numbers that you may find are the industry lab tests where they stack a column of water (measured in millimeters) on a square meter of fabric for a 24-hour period to see when the water and its weight will find a way through. This waterproofness is expressed as "mm/24 hours". You may see a number of 10,000 mm/24 hours on a PreCip jacket. On the Gore-Tex Paclite fabric or Pro 2.5 or 3.5 fabric you may see numbers like 28,000 mm/24 hours – almost triple the weather protection. eVent has had numbers like 20,000 mm/24 hours, which will be reflected in the price tag.

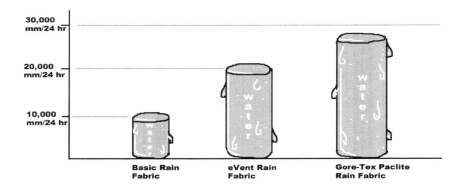

The second lab test is for breathability of the fabric - its ability to allow sweat vapor to exit from a square meter of fabric over the same time period of 24 hours. It's expressed as "g/m²/24 hours". (The "g" stands for grams of sweat vapor.) Since I'm not a lab technician this may have some inaccuracies, but for us hikers it helps to explain why some jackets are $200 to $350 and some are $99. It certainly has for me. The whole dynamic of holding out rain while delivering breathability used to confuse me to where I accepted it on faith, that I wasn't being lied to. That is, until it was explained to me scientifically that a water molecule is nearly 900 times larger than sweat vapor, so having millions of microscopic holes does indeed keep rain (water molecules) at bay while letting sweat vapor escape. If you're wearing a rain jacket and pant while making your miles, you're going to sweat liberally. Even those of you who may sweat very little, no one is immune to being a river of perspiration. So the more advanced the breathability of the fabric, the broader the range of conditions that can be minimized. Since sweat vapor is a whole lot smaller than a water molecule, that's how perspiration can escape while the rain can't get in, but breathability numbers vary like waterproofness.

The PreCip fabric breathability has gotten better, newer numbers put it at 17,000 g/m2/24 hours, which closely mirrors that of Gore-Tex Paclite. Gore-Tex Pro layer options are much higher at 25,000 and EVent at 22,000, thus they have the best performance in breathability. Makers will adjust their products routinely, fabrics will change and improve and fall out of favor. These numbers will change, especially as this book becomes the classic go-to reference for future thru-hikers (fingers crossed)! The purpose of understanding these numbers is to bring clarity of concepts to rain protection.

So why am I giving you all this rocket science mumbo-jumbo? Well, you're not going to be walking to the mall from your car in a polite rain. You'll be living on and walking along mountain ridgelines in all the drama that weather can throw at you. A big difference. If ever there was a reason to own better rain protection, an AT thru-hike would be it. If you can afford the better fabric, get it. If you can't, fret not, I didn't have it on my thru-hikes and still found a smile, albeit a wet one.

Rain jacket and pant design.

My first rain pants had what is called an elastic cuff, a cinched gathering that wraps around your ankle. Do not buy this style. What happens is the rain rolls down the jacket, down the pants and puddles in your socks and shoes. Stupid design. My first rain pants had this design because I didn't know what I needed and didn't know anybody who could look out for me. (But you have me looking out for you.) So when I reached Damascus, Virginia, they got dropped in a hiker box and I bought new ones with a straight cuff, like regular pants.

You want rain pants that have a number of key features. First, you want straight cuffs at the leg bottom like regular pants. This increases the odds that the rain will roll over and off your footwear if they are waterproof. Additionally, some higher end rain pants have a small hook/clip device in the front of the cuff to hook onto your laces to hold them down over your footwear like a gaiter. I absolutely adore this feature. If your pants don't have this feature consider MacGyvering some onto your pair – just take a look at gaiters if you do not understand this little hook concept. Since rain pants are not really a substitute for normal pants, they get pulled on over what you're wearing when weather events appear. Having a longer leg zipper will make for a quicker, easier pull on over your hiking shoes, mids or boots. The bigger your footwear though (mids and boots can limit your ability to flatten out your ankle), the longer you'll want that zipper to be. Rain pant leg zippers vary from about 12 inches to 18 inches to full-length. I prefer the 18inch or better because of that quicker slip on over hiking shoes.

Many of the higher end rain pants and jackets also have articulated leg and arm shapes rather than the straight stove pipe shape. These already mirror our natural bending shape at the knee and elbow, which provides a nice athletic feel.

Rain homage: Forrest Gump could be describing the AT:

> **"One day it started raining, and it didn't quit for four months. We been through every kind of rain there is. Little bitty stingin' rain... and big ol' fat rain. Rain that flew in sideways. And sometimes rain even seemed to come straight up from underneath. Shoot, it even rained at night."**

Other design features important in most all jackets, regardless of the level of fabric performance, is the pit-zip. The pit-zip is the underarm zipper that helps vent your body heat and perspiration from all that huffing and puffing with a loaded pack on. The higher end jackets give you two-way zipper pulls to better place that vent where you want it. You'll also notice that some jacket's front hand pockets are higher than others. This higher position allows you to use them while wearing a backpack hip belt or harness for climbing, where the traditional pocket location would be underneath them, making them unusable. On colder days, if you decide to not use your poles, you can walk with your hands in these higher pockets. And you thought a rain jacket was just a rain jacket?

Since pretty much all rain jackets have hoods your head won't get too wet, but wearing them with all the swish swish noisiness of those fabrics next to your ears takes some getting used to. Hoods sometimes are just hoods - they sit there and when you turn your head, you're now looking at the inside of the hood because it didn't turn with you. Some hoods though have as many as five adjustment options so when you turn your head the hood turns too. The higher-end jackets also have higher-end waterproof zippers. Most zippers on all but the best foul weather gear are not waterproof. Instead they give you an overlapping inch of waterproof fabric to cover the unwaterproof zipper. Isn't that nice of them? All these features are relevant to thru-hiking and will be used, but this extra attention to design is why some foul weather gear is more costly. It's appropriate to again state the cliché here: "You get what you pay for."

When a decision to come off the trail is made (other than from injury or matters at home), usually it is because of very low moments in your emotional strength. Wet conditions and the truly nasty, cold and wet conditions are often the reason. Better foul weather gear is your protection from not only the elements, but also melancholy and despair in some cases. In 2013, the hiker season started out so wet that despite one of the larger thru-hiker starts - nearly 3000 hikers - only a minuscule 13% were able to succeed. That reversed a trend of a thru-hiker success rate averaging about 27% over the last decade. Indeed 2013 was a bad year for hikers trying to earn the moniker of Thru-Hiker.

"There's no one-way to go backpacking."

Since there's no one-way to go backpacking, use this information as you wish. Your thru-hike will face all the weather texture you can conjure up and maybe some you can't, but for the most part foul weather gear is there to keep you dry and keep you warm. For this reason, I'm not a fan of ponchos for an AT thru-hike. Oh, they're great for walking around Disney during a rainstorm, but on a ridgeline with high wind or wind-blown rain, nothing beats full rain gear. My call is to carry full protection.

If you can, invest in premium rain protection for the AT.
Cold rain is, and has been, the undoing of many a hiker.

Secret

Happy Hiker Feet.

How feet and footwear become best friends.

The goal for any hiker is to have feet, footwear and forward motion living in harmony. It is quite clear to anyone wanting to travel a great distance afoot that if the feet aren't happy the hiker won't be making much progress.

From our very first steps in life to a life upright, rarely has our time vertical led us to pondering our footwear like the moments leading up to a thru-hike. Suburbia has taught us, more out of habit, just try some shoes on and if the feeling is acceptable, walk with it.

One of the first mistakes most hikers make is in the buying process. When asked, "What size are you?" most will give their city shoe size not knowing that their hiking shoe size is larger. It's to be expected, though. When you spend all your time on civilized surfaces that are flat, smooth, and paved, why would any of us understand how dynamics like gravity and the act of going downhill could be anything but joyful? When buying hiking footwear, you'll want either a half size to full size larger. Additionally, when foot measurements are taken in a footwear department, make sure it's done while standing – feet can widen or lengthen under your weight. Stand with legs even and your posture straight. What you've bought in the past is irrelevant; you're about to go up and down Mt. Everest more than sixteen times.

When going down mountain, gravity, despite a firm lacing, will force your feet to slide forward with every step. Since mountains by definition are rather large objects, this could mean walking down mountain for miles with your toenails slamming into the front of the toe box. Very painful. By having shoes longer than your city size, your tender toes have enough space to prevent this traumatic slamming. Hiker toenails are happy.

If the slamming does take place for miles and miles, you may see a toenail or two turn black within the week. In a month, the now dead, black nail will just fall off into your sock. The whole blackening and falling off isn't painful, it's the slamming that is. Of course there is a silver lining to a nail falling off...less to carry!

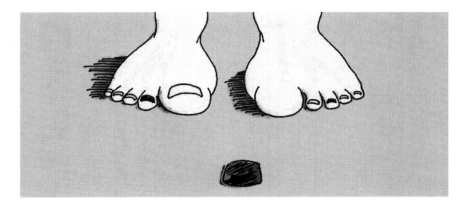

Another common error when one is heading out on a hiking adventure is to think he or she must own high, full leather boots. Many, out of a default way of speaking, say "Hiking Boots" as if the word "boot" is married to the word "hiking". Only the experienced outdoorsy person knows there are also hiking Mids and Shoes and even something called Trail Runners.

(The whole trail runner category is a mess actually since it contains minimalist footwear that offers little toe or underfoot protection to toothy, stiffer running shoes that keep the ounces down on the foot while delivering much of the lateral stability hikers enjoy for carrying a backpack. This disparity in labeling results in confusion, so understand that not all "trail runners" are appropriate to tackle the constant assault from the AT. To be frank, minimalist trail runners won't last much past 300 miles, so seven pairs may be required if chosen. Other trail runners similar to hiking shoes will not need replacing until the 600 to 750 mile range – sort of depends on the grit and abrasiveness of that trail section.)

Once I deciphered for myself what design features enhance our efforts to go backpacking and what aspects are folly, I was able to accomplish two AT thru-hikes, a ton of training miles and time spent on the PCT, a total of more than 5000 miles without a blister. Add in another 5000 miles of running in that same ten-year span, also without a blister, and you have some proven wisdom. I don't have a MD in orthopedics, but rather a more practical footwear education from The School of Hard Walks.

One of my favorite things while on the trail is to observe how different each of us walks (or limps, in some cases). Sure it's one foot in front of the other, but spending a fair amount afoot in the last several years has me more attuned to someone's gait, stride, step, slide, shuffle, saunter, bounce, spring, heel-toe, toe-heel, limps, sore knees, twisted ankle, tendonitis, pronation, supination and resupply pack weights. It's endless. Of course it all stems from the pelvic-bone connecting to the hipbone connecting to the leg, knee, shin, ankle, whatever bone.

Your walk says a lot about you. You can't help but easily spot the confident person simply by watching his or her deliberate pace. Or the timid soul with slow, somewhat small steps. On the trail most of us can determine if we're walking behind a man or woman based on the size of the tread print. I've been able to fine-tune this a bit to know if the person had tuna or peanut butter at their snack break. On good days I can also determine their sock fluff.

We get familiar with hikers in front of us through their tread prints, and in some ways become connected to the individual after days of following that tread pattern in the dirt, even though having never met. To you their tread design is like a fingerprint. Eventually, by the randomness of life on the trail, a face is put to that tread and you feel you know them, sort of. Of course, they haven't any of your connection since those in front have zero knowledge of those behind.

The craziest prints I've followed on the AT weren't shoe prints at all but rather barefoot prints. (What?) Two thousand miles of rocks, stumps and abrasive surfaces is hard enough with shoes, but fleshy tender toes and soles naked without protection? Well, a bag of hammers has a higher IQ.

It's a great time to be a foot.

Many of you may think the requirement for hiking over 500, 1000, or 2000 miles comes down to having the right (and left) hiking boots. However, the modern hiking trend to go lighter with gear has led to footwear changes. With the lightweight gear revolution being in full bloom for over a decade, pack loads in the 50 pound range have become more rare. Nowadays, the modern thru-hiker load is closer to the 30 pound neighborhood. This has allowed us to make changes to our footwear, a place of hidden weight burden. The switch to trail runners or low hiking shoes rather than those heavier leather boots is increasing the odds of succeeding. The combination of heavy boots to handle heavy pack weights lead to a thru-hike success rate of 10%. Said differently, that's a 90% failure rate.

In contrast, the lightening of loads and footwear in lock step has led to a 27% (+/-) success rate. That's quite an improvement in the odds.

Trail runners or low hiking shoes keep our feet nimble and reduce the leg fatigue that comes with weight and distance. Whether the weight is in your pack or on your feet, your body and resolve must still carry it.

"A pound saved on the foot is like five pounds saved from the backpack."

~ Old Hiker Wisdom

If your pack weight is over 35 lbs then maybe a full boot is a helpful tool for the ankles (my opinion). But if your pack is under 35 lbs, then using a boot is more a choice rather than a necessity. Too many falsely assume that a boot will prevent a turned ankle. Let's be clear, you can turn an ankle in nearly any footwear, including a boot. Once your momentum starts to slide out laterally - usually due to losing your balance, not staying in the moment or just the difficulty of the AT landscape - only a well-positioned tree can stop that momentum leading to an ankle turn. This is also why I highly recommend using trekking poles, regardless of your footwear decision of hiking with shoes, mids or boots. Trekking poles offer you stability that can prevent the loss of balance.

What this weight savings means is fairly simple. You'll make your same miles with less effort. You'll have less rubbery legs at the end of the day. You'll be more nimble of foot and leg and may even do it with a quicker pace. Less fatigue means quicker recovery tomorrow, as well as possibly fewer trips and falls from exhausted leg muscles unable to step higher.

What I do love about boots is how lacing them up speaks to high adventure. That the higher the laces go, the more serious I am about attacking the wilderness. Those intangibles are fun and can make one stand taller. Boots, however, are heavier and less nimble, but many of you couldn't dream of wearing anything else. Footwear choices and the discussions of them can be contentious. Ultimately, you should wear what gives you confidence and makes your feet happy. But don't confuse your stubbornness or predisposed opinions with false beliefs on what is required.

Hikers, on average, take 2000 steps per mile.

Revisiting our 2000 steps per mile reality, if one wears footwear that weighs 1 pound per shoe rather than 2 pounds per boot - a weight saving of 2 pounds total, the hiker avoids carrying 2000 pounds in a 1-mile trek (1000 not carried with your left leg and 1000 not carried with your right leg). So let's do the math for a 10-miler, you would avoid carrying 20,000 pounds. Tomorrow when you hike, you avoid another 20,000 pounds, and so on.

10 Miles = 20,000 Steps

Subtracting 1 lb per step is 10,000 lbs not carried on your left leg and 10,000 lbs not carried on your right leg.

Do you think you'd be fresher after one week of 10-mile days if you didn't carry 140,000 pounds? Remarkable stuff, right? Also remember that the AT is a "mountain" footpath, so that is 20,000 pounds not carried up and down and up again rather than on flat ground.

On a 20-mile day - and there'll be some – that means not carrying 40,000 pounds. On a Georgia-to-Maine thru-hike those numbers ramp up to staggering totals. By shaving 2 pounds off your feet on your end-to-end journey (an average of 5 million steps) means avoiding 5 MILLION POUNDS. Think how your odds of posing for a photo by a weather-beaten sign with the word "Katahdin" on it would go up if you didn't have to carry 5 million pounds on your feet?

Go back now with a fresh perspective and look at my "26 Days" chart (page 94) in the Making Miles Is Your Job section. Knowing what you know now, it's a bit easier to see how an ordinary, middle-aged man could make such remarkable progress.

Footwear will never guarantee your success at thru-hiking, but it can reduce the burden of the journey. And a reduced burden of weight will be evident in the width of your smile and the depth of your emotional strength. It all helps. The math is fairly amazing and sheds light on how less weight, be it in your pack or on your legs, helps to reduce the burden of gravity acting on that weight.

Footwear destruction is guaranteed.

Almost any kind of shoe can be worn the entire length of a thru-hike if one doesn't mind wearing tatters or slipping on every surface. The decision to switch out to a new pair always comes down to tread stickiness for me. Fret not the split seam or torn fabric, those will not affect the tread performance. Oh sure, you'd like your footwear to be invincible, but the AT will

My first journey's shoes became a great memento for the yard.

destroy whatever you put on your feet. A split seam in the stitching will most times create a more comfortable shoe since it often occurs at a high contact point by your foot. Naturally you want your wingtips or pumps to be perfect looking for your pose clothes in suburbia, but hiking footwear is going through the harshest of environments. Tread stickiness and your comfort should be your top criteria for a change out.

I went through three pairs on my first thru-hike and four pairs on my second end-to-end journey.

On thru-hike #1 my first shoes got changed out after 600 miles, the second after a 1000 (they were in tatters) and the third took me to the summit of Mt. Katahdin.

All the shoes were purchased before I started and just waited with my other maildrops until they were needed.

On thru-hike #2 my first shoes went to the 650 mile range, the second to about 800. In Vermont I went to a lighter trail runner with softer, stickier tread compound, but after crossing into the State of Maine the next morning I slipped on black ice (in August!) and broke my wrist. After a 29 day delay, I continued my hike with a new, fourth pair, just in case that third pair was unlucky (one never knows) and reached the summit of Katahdin. No traditional hiking footwear would have handled the black ice unless some sort of Yaktrax or crampons were on them. Then again, it was the first week of August when heat and humidity are the norm - who would've ever imagined black ice would be anywhere on the length of the AT in the summer?

Marley, an '06 trail mate, only got a few hundred miles in his first pair, that's when he came to the trails first river ford. Smartly, to keep his socks dry (a man after my own heart), Marley removed his socks and shoes and with laces tied together draped them over his neck before wading in wearing his Crocs. But alas, river bottoms are filled with nooks and crannies and wildlife. It is there, in the middle of the stream that a rather large crawdad (we suspect) grabbed his colorful Croc. Marley wobbled but remained vertical; unfortunately the body dip caused a trapeze action that sent his sock-stuffed hiking shoes into the river. Whether bad luck or some crazy gravitational alignment of the planets, Marley's shoes bounced rather than sank. The now floating trail shoes-turned-canoes found the current and bid Marley good luck on his journey. They had decided to go with the flow – next stop, The Atlantic Ocean. The remaining 80 miles to town were in Crocs. Even with the best of precautions, stuff happens during a thru-hike.

Fording.

My counsel on fords: I have a different strategy for you to consider when facing a ford along the AT, most of which are in Maine. First, you'll want to reconnoiter the stream to find smoother, slower flowing water. Pinches in the landscape cause river bottoms to deepen due to the faster flowing water. An area with smoother water generally means a shallower, slower flow, albeit wider crossing. Second, once a crossing place is determined, take off your hiking shoes and remove your socks. Then put your hiking shoes back on (sockless) and lace firmly. By using your hiking shoes, you'll have better footing than with your camp shoes (Crocs) or barefoot. Third, angle yourself so you're facing upstream to see any debris that may be heading your way. Unbuckle your hip belt and sternum strap so a quicker exit from your pack can happen in the event of falling; a heavy wet pack caught in a current can lead to tragedy. Your trekking poles will be extremely valuable here to provide extra points of balance on what are usually awkward bottoms with limited visibility. Now step in and ford.

Once to the other side, pour the water out of your shoes, beat a bit more water out against a rock or tree and then put the dry socks back on and re-lace. Of course the sock liners and socks will get damp from the wetness inside your shoes, but they won't be soaked. This will be the least annoying of the options while still providing good footing.

Choosing your hiking footwear.

When making progress in backpacking requires us to have happy hiker feet, we start to ponder footwear a bit more than our suburban days of wearing wingtips, loafers, heels and wedges. The first design characteristic that helps your stride is:

Rocker Sole. A rocker sole is easily spotted on any footwear wall by the pronounced curve between the heel and toe. Like the rails on a rocking chair, your natural stride is to rock from heel strike to midfoot then to a forefoot lift off. Having a sole that curves between the heel and toe allows your footwear to naturally rock with your stride. In fact, if the profile of your sole has an arc like a smile, so will you. If you look at the footwear on the image below, you'll notice how the shoe curves up at the toe and heel and how it is squared off and flat on the boot.

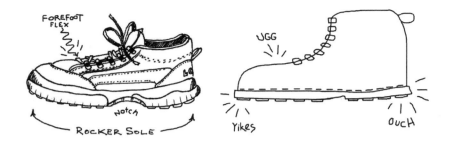

There was a time when finding a rocker sole in your hiking footwear was difficult; full leather boots would routinely square off the heel and toe area. This old school design resulted in footwear that resisted what your foot wanted to do naturally: rock. With the sole squared off and your foot wanting to rock, feet tended to lift and rub the inside, and we all know what those friction spots led to.

Countless creative lacing techniques were invented to try to hold your foot still in a shoe that didn't want to rock. Can you say "painful break-in period"?

Forefoot Flex is as important as a rocker sole. Together, these two design characteristics help your feet and shoes to avoid fights and live in harmony. Just look at how your forefoot area flexes in your stride before lifting off to the other foot. The more forefoot flex your hiking footwear has the lower the odds of blisters on your heel.

Don't confuse stiffness with stability. Having footwear that is stiff laterally - meaning across the shoe - is good. It gives your ankles and feet stability and a solid platform. We like that feature in hiking where the landscape is never flat. Stiffness from heel to toe is bad. This means resistance to what your foot wants to do in a natural stride, which is to flex and rock. When you have both forefoot flex and rocking sole working together, it's not crazy to go from shoebox to the trail in the same day, and it's not crazy to make mile after mile without any foot issues.

Custom Lacing. Unlike the old lacing concoctions that forced your foot to conform to the shoe rather than the shoe to your foot, the custom lacing I'd like to suggest will help with some common issues. Often when hikers lace up firmly, the tension of the laces can reduce the circulation to our toes, causing them to fall asleep or go tingly – not desired.

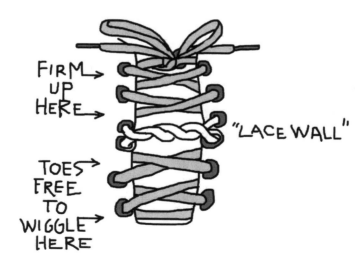

FIRM UP HERE →

"LACE WALL"

TOES FREE TO WIGGLE HERE →

Normally, before you tie a bow in your laces, you first cinch down the laces with an intertwine. If you double that intertwine (a surgeons knot) it forms what I call a "lace wall". Consider putting a double intertwine in the middle of the shoe if you experience circulation cut off and thus tingly toes. A lace wall can be put in anywhere along the laces. After the lace wall is in place just re-lace all the remaining eyelets and tie your normal bow, then double knot your laces. A firm lace up and its tension will not be able to work down beyond that lace wall. This also helps hikers who have a wider forefoot or bunions in this area and want to avoid the crushing pain from a too tight forefoot (me).

Waterproof or Not? Choosing waterproof footwear will have its advantages for an AT thru-hike with its wet muddy trails, wet grasses, morning dew, and wet trailside foliage. All these scenarios along with fending off light rain will be handled when wearing waterproof hiking shoes, mids or boots: Dry socks are a wonderful thing.

Don't for a minute think that wearing waterproof footwear means your feet will stay dry in a thru-hike. Even with full foul weather gear and waterproof shoes, if it rains for hours and hours during the hiking day, everything will be wet. Your shoes will actually become bathtubs, holding the rain. Oh well. Waterproof footwear can fend off light showers, but the real advantage to choosing waterproof footwear over the more breathable non-waterproof is on days *after* the rain where wetness remains. It's one thing to have wet feet during a hard rain, it's completely unacceptable to have wet feet on sunny days after rain events. Since footwear discussions can be quite opinionated, some may argue that during the summer the breathable shoes keep your feet dryer. In the summer, through the Mid-Atlantic States, when the temps are hitting the high 80s and 90s with humidity in the same range, you'll be sweating like a waterfall and your socks will be pretty moist from perspiration running down your legs. Whatever your decision, it's not irreparable and can be amended.

Size matters, support, and cushioning. Size matters if you like having toenails. To revisit a previous mention, your hiking shoe size is a half to full size larger than your business/city shoe size. This larger size, along with a good lacing, helps prevent gravity from slamming our toenails into the end of the shoe (painful) on the long down-mountains.

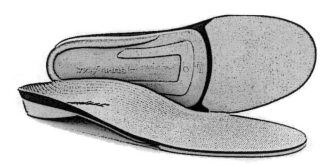

Having hiking footwear of a larger size holds other benefits, such as extra volume to add better insoles and cushioning. Normally, the insoles that come with our hiking shoes are wimpy cushion ones that offer no support to the demands of hiking 500 to 700 miles per shoe. During the stride, your foot tends to focus all the impact of you and your pack weight on just two parts of your foot, the heel and forefoot. The wimpy cushion insoles fail to offer any support through the mid-foot or arch. This results in a trampoline effect on every step. Add up those steps - 2000 per mile - and your feet may be more tired and sore than they have to be.

By adding a rigid, stable insole like those made by SuperFeet or Sole, the arch gets some well-deserved attention and the trampoline effect is reduced. I used SuperFeet on both of my thru-hikes, but I also did something they didn't recommend. I added yet another insole of just cushioning with my rigid SuperFeet. Hiking shoes notoriously omit good cushioning straight from the factory, which makes absolutely no sense. We're walking on rugged terrain with extra weight on our bodies covering distances much greater than the typical distance from parking lot to mall. Ten, 15, 20, 25, even 30 mile days means a whole bunch of foot impacts. One would think some good cushioning would have benefits. Just like a rigid insole can help, so does adding cushioning.

Today, a whole host of rigid insoles are available from nearly every athletic shoemaker. Experiment. Remember, if your feet and footwear aren't best friends, you won't be going very far.

Sliding in an old running shoe insole of cushioning underneath the rigid Superfeet or Sole can easily be tried before the hike.

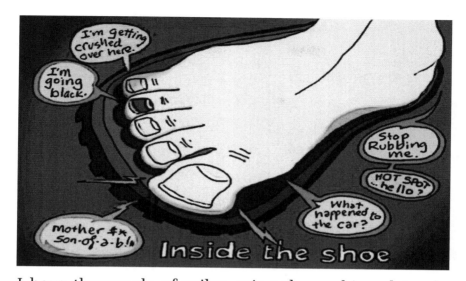

I have thousands of miles using the cushioned insole on top of my rigid insole and thousands of miles with it the other way around. Experiment to see which softens your stride best. During my thru-hikes, before I discovered that Spenco makes a flat, closed-cell foam cushion layer (green and black) that last forever and won't absorb water, I used the crappy Dr. Scholl's Double-Pillow insoles you get at drug stores. They completely "pack down" in just a few days, thus losing their cushioning properties. They also absorb water. But they were readily available along the AT during town stops and were cheap dollar-wise. (Come to think about it, they were cheap quality wise, too.) I'd buy a new pair each town visit since they were just a few bucks. My feet were worth it. The Spenco option would have been a far superior choice if I'd known about them on my first hike.

One thing to be cautious in adding cushioning is make sure the cushioning is flat without the raised heel. Many sold today have the raised heel - not good since this changes your posture.

SuperFeet finally got smart and added the "Orange" to their insole line, which combines cushioning and rigid arch support. Softer striding can now be more easily attained for your thru-hike than all the shenanigans and hoops I had to go through.

Socks Are Strategic. Cotton may be the fabric of life but it's the enemy of the outdoors. Cotton socks stay wet, dry slowly, lose their shape by folding over, increase friction hot spots and hold odor. While cotton socks are lovely for city dwellers, they will bring unhappy feet to hikers.

You want wool or synthetic socks. I've become particularly smitten with the Darn Tough Merino Wool socks as of late. Made in Vermont, they employ modern design by using different thicknesses in different areas of the sock for improved performance. Gone are the days of rag socks that are coarse and thick everywhere because that's how they did it 1100 years ago.

Merino wool in socks better regulates body temperature. They are warm in the cold, cool in the hot, and avoids the itchy old days. With improved, more thoughtful design, socks have become high art and we hikers get the benefits.

REI's synthetic multi-sport socks also use this modern thinking and also work well. REI's classic wool hiking socks and SmartWool's choices have successfully made it end to end on the AT countless times. The newer SmartWool PhD Outdoor socks are worth considering since they too have the progressive thicknesses similar to the Darn Tough. Wigwam, Dahlgren, Thorlo, are all nice too (aren't I being just wonderfully politically correct and sock generous?). Just say no to cotton hiking socks and save "The fabric of life" for your BBQ party clothes.

High mileage perspiration and/or wet days are why I always use sock liners. Once the soft fluffy nap of the sock is wet, the odds of friction go up. A sock liner becomes a buffering layer to that friction. By wearing liners the hiking sock will rub against the liner rather than your foot skin. I use them and haven't had a blister issue in 5000 AT miles. I recommend you use them.

You might also consider using your liner with a midweight or lightweight hiking sock rather than the standard heavyweight sock. The thinner weight hiking socks do just as fine a job when coupled with a liner in my mileage laboratory experiments, and your spare set in the pack weighs less. The lightweight socks can also reduce foot perspiration.

The Tongue Wedge (That's what I call it) or Under-Lace Thingamajig might also be apt. It is a triangular piece of dense foam that you slip between your laces and your shoe's tongue to reduce the internal volume. What it does is help prevent your foot from being forced into the toe box on those long down-mountains. A tongue wedge is a band-aid fix to already owning shoes that are a bit too short. Candidly, there probably isn't any fix to a short shoe on a thru-hike other than cutting out the front end, which creates new problems: broken toes. You should replace them with a bigger shoe before you start.

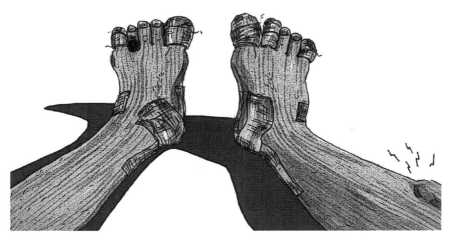

Avoid going too far too fast with too much too soon. Your exuberance will be raging, but body parts need a few weeks to acclimate to the demands.

Secret

Keep it easy, find it easy peasy.

I once witnessed a hiker turn his backpack upside down upon arrival at a shelter. What fell out was about 40 Ziplocs carrying all his stuff – each the same color, same size, making finding this-that-and-the-other-thing, well, slow. I've also witnessed hikers pack up in the morning with no particular method and hike on a mile or so, and then realize their sleeping bag was back at the shelter.

A small degree of organization in one's pack can add quickness to finding things both in camp and during the day. The placement of some items in the pack can add to an easier daily choreography.

If you're new to backpacking, you may have labored over your decision on which backpack will have the most pockets – I see it often in the store. Most long-distance savvy hikers forego these pack features and opt for a lighter, simpler top loading pack with just one large compartment. When you open your pack roughly seven to nine times a day for 180 days, you realize that a simpler way to see, find, and quickly get to everything adds ease to your passage. To that end, consider organizing the entire trip's gear in six stuff sacks, each a different color - this will provide quick recognition of items. Additionally, by employing a strategy of "grouping" gear by time of day or function, you'll have everything you need when a stuff sack is picked up. The six bag concept is as follows:

      1) Daytime Food bag

      2) Night bag

      3) Everything Else bag

      4) Clothes bag

      5) Dinner Food bag

      6) Water Filter bag

Of course your sleeping bag and tent have their own bags and your sleeping pad may be bagless if using closed-cell foam, otherwise it has its own bag if an inflatable.

Let's discuss grouping in relation to your Dinner Food Bag. First off, the dinner food bag needs to be a waterproof bag. We do not sleep with our food when hammocking, tenting or using a tarp. Our food hangs in a tree away from where we sleep and, since thunderstorms can come in at 2 am, it must keep our food dry and in good shape. In addition to all our dinners, this bag will hold our stove, pot, fuel and spork. When cooking and eating is done, our 50 feet of paracord used to hang the bag is in there too. Since I like to have the ambiance of a campfire, my fire starters are also in that same bag; I usually start the campfire task while dinner is cooking. When picking up that one bag - mine is a Sea To Summit 20 liter Ultra-Sil dry bag - I get my dinners and hot chocolate and cookies for afterward, my kitchen to cook the dinner, the ability to hang it afterwards and to do so by a campfire. That is grouping and, apparently, many haven't thought of it. I learned it from a hiker on the AT before my first thru-hike and then took it further by applying it to everything. Instead of gathering all the items from different pockets, it all lives together, grouped by the time of day it will be used.

In the same vain of the Dinner Food Bag, I created The Night Bag. It contains everything that I'd use every night in camp. A small bag of a different color, it holds my headlamp, spare batteries in a Ziploc, reading glasses for writing and guidebook planning, music device, lip balm, Bag Balm foot rub and chafe soother (1 oz tin) and my toothbrush and paste. When I arrive in camp, whether shelter or tenting, I'll claim a spot in the shelter by placing my Tyvek ground sheet down, then I'll lay my sleeping pad down and pull out my sleeping bag to start lofting up. Then I take off my hiking shoes, give my feet a Bag Balm foot rub and slip on my spare sock liners and camp shoes. My hiking shoes get placed by my sleeping bag hood and the Night Bag gets set in the shoes (if they're not wet from the day). The food bag will get set aside and other clothes will get put on. Chores then commence – water harvesting, preparations for dinner and the like. When Hikers' Midnight comes (sunset), I'll grab the headlamp from my Night Bag there by my sleeping bag. The backpack has been emptied and is hanging on a hook in the shelter or when tenting, the now flat backpack will be at the head end of my tent to help aid in acting like a pillow. The real pillow will be my Clothes Bag.

The Everything Else Bag is everything you hope you never need such as first aid, extra bite valve, etc. Once again a different color from the rest and of the lightest weight ripstop nylon. Here is a list of some those extra things and first aid:

· *After Bite - Anti itch pen for bug bites*
· *Sting Eze - Sting pain stopper if stung*
· *Pepto Tablets*
· *Lip Balm (extra)*
· *Allergy meds (eyes & nose)*
· *First Aid paper tape (works better than duck tape on feet)*

Repair items and helpful extras:

- *Tent pole splint*
- *Two 18" Velcro Straps (for "what if's")*
- *Needle and thread (already threaded)*
- *Extra Bite Valve*
- *Whistle*
- *Duck tape – 18–24 inches wrapped on each trekking pole*

The Water Filter Bag also holds my 2-liter foldable Platypus bottle for holding my dinner water when I make camp. Upon arriving in camp or shelter, after a spot is claimed with my sleeping pad and bag, I pull out my 3-liter Platypus Hoser reservoir from my backpack and grab my Water Filter Bag and mosey down to the water source to relax and harvest. Also in this bag is some of my electrolyte powder or tablets, which get added to my 3-liter reservoir for drinking throughout the night. When I pump water during the hiking day the electrolytes are right there to be added. Once again: grouping.

The Daytime Food Bag holds all my breakfasts (Muscle Milk powder) and milkshaker, lunch foods and extra electrolytes to add during refilling of my reservoir mid day. The Daytime Food Bag is the last stuff sack to get packed in the morning, thus sitting at the top for quick access on numerous snack breaks during the day. No reason to bury it deep when you know you'll be reaching for it multiple times a day. And since food is usually our heaviest stuff, it breaks up the load. This 10-liter bag of yet another color gets dropped inside the larger water-proof 20-liter Dinner Food Bag when it's time to hang it.

Your Clothes Bag obviously holds your dry second outfit. It does not hold your foul weather gear since rain events can sneak up on you. Those get placed in the outside stretch pocket in the center of most packs. Rain jacket and pants, rain cover, and my wind shirt all rest together in that outside, easily accessible pocket. At bedtime, with a small adjustment to what clothes are in the bag, it now becomes your pillow. If your hiking outfit is wet from the day, they get hung on whatever nail is available in the shelter to drip – everyone wants to be in a shelter on a rainy day – so unused nails will be hard to come by. Do not hold any hope that your clothes will be dry by morning if the rain continues throughout the night. The wetness in the clothes has no place to move to when the air is saturated with a high dew point from continued rain. A cold, wet dressing of the still-wet clothing will be your fate in the morning – an act I absolutely hated.

That's nearly the whole kit-and-caboodle, in just six lightweight stuff sacks of different colors. The moment you look in the pack there's instant recognition of where everything is. Effortless. My pack also has two outer side pockets and two hip belt pockets, so let's discuss those.

In one side pocket of my pack is my toilet paper, hey nature calls. Ok, stop your snickering. There are obviously some topics on a thru-hike that have to be addressed before they are faced. Toilet paper may top that list. Before you are the requirements one could need for a five-month adventure: Thirty half rolls that have been de-tubed, so they'll fold flat and squeeze into a quart-size Ziploc. That's one for each maildrop. Now, I actually don't think you'll need that many half rolls, but it's definitely one of those things you'll wish you had and didn't use, rather than needed and didn't have. Leaves and pinecones just aren't cuddly soft now, are they? (Use your imagination if you don't have first hand knowledge.)

As we all know, not all TP is created equal. Their quality sort of separates the budget-minded from the luxury hiker. Some TP, such as you find in gas station restrooms and cheap motels, is usually single-ply, semi-transparent and disintegrates in your hand. However, it's very economical and can be purchased at Big Lots in packs of 78 rolls for $1.23. (And boy do you get your money's worth!)

If you're a luxury hiker and want TP that is thick, soft and fluffy, you have to put your money where your tush is. The Mercedes Benz of TP is Charmin. But opinions vary.

Every season, thru-hikers have a bad habit of stealing rolls of the valuable commodity from town – cafés and motel stops – which does little towards making a good impression with the owners. It's always the little things that create the biggest annoyances. Stealing TP isn't exactly trying to be a good citizen or an AT ambassador along the journey, and it can lead to hikers no longer being welcomed.

TP wasn't always important to me. Once during high school, a few of us "rolled" another of our friend's houses at three in the morning for his birthday. He woke to see the handiwork of what two hours and 174 rolls of toilet paper can do to a front yard. Since my thrus, I now have a fondness for the stuff.

Although having TP is quite practical, I've experienced the oddest sense of power from loading in a big, new half-roll in the backpack side pocket. Heading out of town, back to the mountain forest with a fat fluffy roll makes me walk a bit taller, ready for another week, ready for all that awaits. Who would have ever thought that TP could touch us in such a sensitive spot?

When drinking 4 to 6 liters of water day after day while doing long periods of moderate activity, the human body becomes quite regular in the "doing your business" category. It also results in a quick trigger. Consider placing your TP in one of those outer side pack pockets. Let it have its own quart Ziploc (because it rains even while doing your business), and then keep that in a gallon Ziploc. Inside that same gallon Ziploc, I grouped three other small snack-size Ziplocs. One had my Excedrin, another my Mega-Man multi-vitamins (which I took every morning) and the third had my Tylenol PM (which I took every night). TP and the aspirin could routinely be needed daily; having them in the outer pocket but double Ziploc'd provided quick access.

On the opposite side of your pack is usually another side pocket. It is here that another gallon Ziploc holds guidebook data pages and profiles.

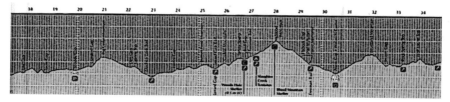

The guidebook pages are for things considered data: distances to water, towns, motels, laundry, and food. Of course, I usually refer to those things simply as water, towns, motels, laundry, and food, but if you want to sound smart and official, call it data. Every rest break, you can check the profiles to where you are, what has been done and what the future holds. This accessible side pocket location allows for better decision-making like whether your legs still have enough juice to move farther. Each of my maildrops had the relevant data pages and profiles for that next section, limiting the paperweight. Today's new guidebooks finally wised up and have profiles synched to the data mileage. Brilliant! My profiles are from the waterproof paper, big topo maps that came in those state by state sets. Only I cut the profiles out of the topo and only carried them – they're bigger than the profiles included in the guide-books. I like that.

In the same side pack pocket that holds my data I kept my Tyvek ground cloth (30 inches by 7 ft) I used under my 1-person tent and as a shelter floor cloth to keep my sleeping bag a bit cleaner. If carrying a tent footprint, keep it here. This allows you to use it during the day at break time as a picnic cloth to keep yourself cleaner. As the bug season kicks in, spray this Tyvek or tent foot-print with Permethrin and it will repel ticks and other critters for a month and a half (42 days). Permethrin is odorless and can be sprayed on your clothing (lasting and repelling critters for up to 6 washes) or on your stuff – backpack, sleeping bag or whatever - to keep them away. It is NOT for you, it is for your stuff. Deet and Picaridin is for you. The George Patton planner side of me says to have more sent further along the trail for re-spraying after a month and a half to keep it working strong and keeping yourself tick free.

In one of my hip-belt pockets I kept a head net in case I walked myself into a swarm of gnats and mosquitos. Having a head net can be the difference from having a comfortable snack break or going insane when they descend on you when not moving. A small spray bottle of 30% Deet also lived in that hip pocket. However, if starting a southbound thru-hike I'd recommend Picaridin since it is a touch more effective against the black fly you'll discover in the early June hatching. In the other I had my waterproof camera, my custom Hiker To Town bandana for a quick communiqué with a passing car, and the hiker's best friend early in the journey: Body Glide chafe stopper.

Grouping and placement of items that could be used frequently in accessible locations - daytime food bag at the top rather than buried deep in a pack - makes for an efficient use of time and an easier passage.

This now leaves just a few items vital to the journey: my plastic. In its own quart size Ziploc is my hiker wallet, which is also kept in the larger gallon Ziploc holding the maps. Let's see, there's the ATM card so I don't have to carry a wad of cash – although I do tend to carry several hundred in tens and fives. You never know when you'll need your Social Security card, although having one has never made me secure socially. There's my REI membership card that isn't actually needed since anyone can walk in to purchase wilderness-conquering doodads. My MasterCard, as in "Charge it" is fairly important even though it really means "Delay it". And maybe the most important item for one named "Postcard" is my Creative License. Every visit to a store, diner, whatever, you can grab your Ziploc hiker wallet out of the larger map

Ziploc. Hiking the AT means you need important stuff to have multiple lines of defense against the elements.

Stuffing all those stuff sacks in your pack.

Conceptually, there's a way to load your pack that will help you have better balance by keeping your center of gravity close to your spine. This will help with footing and posture as well. You want lighter weight gear on the bottom and lighter weight gear on the top, with the heaviest items, usually food and water, in the middle close to your back. Put the heavy items at the bottom, and the pack feels like it's drooping on your butt. Load the pack with the heavy items up high, and the pack wobbles more than it has to. Having the heavier items close to your back and in the middle will help make the load feel better physically while keeping your feet nimble with good balance.

Because I split my food bag into two, no one bag was overwhelming. Here's where those bags lived inside:

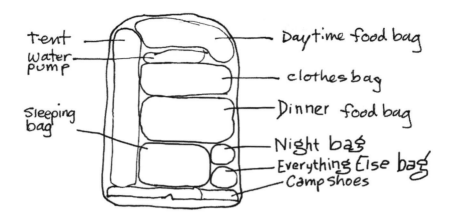

Tent
water
pump

Sleeping
bag

Daytime food bag

clothes bag

Dinner food bag

Night bag
Everything Else bag
Camp shoes

Now some of you are wondering where my sleeping pad is in this sketch. I used the Therm-a-Rest Z Lite accordion fold closed-cell foam pad. It comes from the factory with 14 panels on a 6 ft length. For my purposes though, I reduced that to six panels – enough to cover my heaviest contact points of shoulder to butt. Rather than accordion folding it after each panel, I folded it only once after three panels, thus making it just two layers thick. This allowed me to slide it down inside the pack at the back area and then all the stuff sacks got loaded. It never looked like I even had a pad until unpacking at camp. Each morning's pack up had to start with my pad and then move from bottom to top. This provided an order that kept me from forgetting things, like that one hiker who forgot his sleeping bag. Find a loading order that makes sense for you and stick to it.

My top tips for taming the tough.

1) All stuff sacks of different colors with items "grouped" as pointed out.

2) Food hanging rope (also known as your bear rope) with a small rock bag and carabineer. Attach 50 ft of 3 to 4mm thin paracord to a small bag (baseball size). Knot in a carabiner on the rope about 3 inches from the bag. Coil rope and stow in the bag. When hanging food bag, uncoil some slack, put a rock in the bag and underhand it over a limb. Attach waterproof food bag to carabineer and tie off to another tree. Ideal hang is to have food bag 8 ft off the ground, 6 ft out from the main tree trunk and about 4 ft below the hang limb. It doesn't guarantee something won't get it, but it sure beats sleeping with all those delicious goodies.

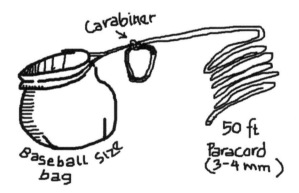

3) The other end of the rope can become a spare shoelace.

4) Step deep when climbing boulders or rock steps. Rocks can teeter no matter their weight or size. Step deep to the mountainside of the rock to minimize a tread slip and knee slam. On descents, step shallow to the mountainside rather than the edge.

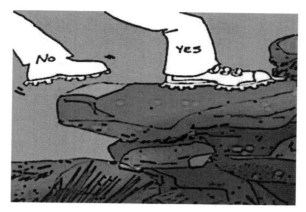

5) Never hunt for your spork string: Attach to the top of your food bags 12 inches of thin cord with a tiny clip or carabiner at the other end for clipping your spork to it. No food bag scavenger hunt.

6) Never lose your tiny pocketknife string: Same as previous, but sew a string to the inside bottom of your hiking pants pocket and let your knife live there. I used the Swiss Army Knife keychain model at 1 ounce.

7) Keep tent footprint or Tyvek ground sheet (30 inches X 7 ft) in the outside pack pocket for rest breaks. I found this size Tyvek was enough to help safeguard my 1 person tent floor and not too big to be piggish when claiming a spot on the shelter floor.

8) Spray the ground sheet or footprint with the odorless Permethrin to repel ticks and critters for a month and a half. You can also use on your other items like hat, backpack, and sleeping bag to keep the nasties from hopping on you when you're taking breaks on the ground. Especially helpful through NJ, NY, CT and MA when the mosquitos get bad. (When sprayed in clothing

it will repel insects through 6 washes ...say Whaaat!) Permethrin is for your stuff, not your skin. Use Deet or Picardin (which is more effective against biting black fly if you're up north in early June when the nasties hatch) for your skin.

9) Hand letter in bold font "Hiker To Town" with a black Sharpie on that Tyvek or on a bandana for quicker hitch-hikes to town (as shown earlier). That thumb of yours when pointing up also works well, telling everyone you're ready for burgers, showers, and laundry. Expect Towners with pickups to be the most likely to stop and expect hopping in the truck bed rather than the cab.

10) Hiker To Town bandana with Velcro sewn in the corners. I attached Velcro counterparts on my trekking poles so the bandana can be a taut billboard and stand by itself when poles are driven into the ground. Once again a Sharpie will work for the lettering, only the letters need to be bold and big.

11) Avoid the water reservoir bulge in your backpack. Use a 3-liter reservoir in your backpack, but only put 2-liters of water in it. This will allow the water to flatten out in the extra volume, eliminating the pressure of the fully filled "bulge" reservoir your other gear will be pressing against.

12) Music and earphones to drown out snoring hikers or sounds of mice. Choose music that compliments the adventure, such as Mary Chapin Carpenter's "10,000 Miles" rather than Green Day anything. Consider music

with grandeur like *The Magnificent Seven* Theme by Elmer Bernstein or the theme to *Last of the Mohicans* movie, even some Sinatra "In The Wee Small Hours" of the morning. Let the music bring the day to a soft landing – my two cents. Otherwise, have earplugs if music isn't desired.

13) If music earphones aren't wireless, but have a traditional cord attached to the device and one spins as they sleep, put the music device on your head under your fleece hat so the cord doesn't wrap around your neck (me, true story, many times).

14) Unzip all pack pockets so mice can go in and out without consequence if you happen to leave a morsel or crumb inside.

15) Duck Tape wrapped on trekking poles. I use 18 inches to two feet on each pole. The one body part that can atrophy on a thru-hike are the arm muscles. Might as well give them something to carry.

16) In both food bags, keep a gallon Ziploc for trash. As it gets full, keep both in the top of your pack for opportunistic trash can sightings. Dump the trash, keep the Ziploc.

17) Use a waterproof 20-liter dry bag for your food bag. We do not sleep with our food, and rain comes in at 2 am.

18) The same dry bag of a different color protects your sleeping bag beautifully. Use the stuff sack that came

with your sleeping bag first to make it compact and then drop that into the 20 liter dry bag. Just squeeze the air out of the dry bag to keep it compact.

19) In an AT shelter, orient your head to the open front edge with feet facing to the inside. Mice like to run around the inside perimeter of the shelter and not so much the exposed front. Also, there's a better breeze on the front edge. During colder months you can reverse it to cut down on the colder breeze.

20) Electrolytes in your hiking water. Tablets or powder can improve endurance and hydration while helping to prevent leg cramps. Drink liberally and make your miles. The better tasting your water, the more of it you'll drink – a good thing.

21) Dryer sheet in your clothes bag. Put a Fabreeze or scented dryer sheet in for a fresher scent. The clothes bag will be your pillow, so having something that smells good near your nose is nice.

22) After a month of sweating into your backpack and some of it seeping into your stuff sacks, you'll want to include them with your laundry to get the "gamey" quality out of them.

23) On climbs, slow your pace and maintain a steady stepping, breathing, and poling pace. Consider my silent chant of "Don't…stop…'til…the…top. Don't stop 'til the top, etc." One word per step helps with focus and distraction to the pain of some ascents. This keeps the blood in the climbing muscles while minimizing your

chances of getting too winded. The result is reaching the summit without stopping. Upon reaching the summit at that slower pace, consider continuing that slow pace as a "rest walk" to recover instead of stopping. Small adjustments will result in better mileage and the expansion of your fitness envelope.

24) Step over stuff rather than onto it. Or go around, but avoid all the extra impact that come from the step-downs attacking the knees, joints, and increasing the odds of slips. Wet wood can be more slippery than black ice.

25) Wide mouth pee bottle with secure cap. When you've just got to go and it's raining cats and dogs, a pee bottle can help. Women can use a Freshette Urinary Director with their pee bottle. Since I'm prone to leg cramps after long mileage days, I'd rather be wet than risk getting a cramp in my tent while peeing. A light Gatorade bottle can often work.

26) Bandana on your pack shoulder strap for excessive sweat.

27) On wet, slippery surfaces, shorten your stride length to keep your center of gravity tighter to your leg balance. An ounce of prevention and caution might be the difference between becoming a Thru-Hiker or going home with an injury.

28) Put small dollops of silicone on your sleeping pad to help keep yourself from slipping off it as you toss and turn at night.

These are all things that have added ease and value to my hikes. Now for a few that others used that didn't.

A) Put your wet shirt under your sleeping pad at night to speed drying time from your warmth. Nope, didn't work. Nothing dries if the air is filled with moisture; the wetness has no place to evaporate.

B) Use a foil space blanket bag to slide your sleeping bag into for added warmth. This works, but it is so noisy it will be like sleeping on a bag of potato chips. You'll make such a racket you may get kicked out of the shelter. And those bags will never, ever, fold back up small.

C) Stretching your socks over a Nalgene bottle to speed drying. What this really accomplishes is stretching out your socks so they don't fit well anymore.

D) Placing your leather footwear close to the campfire for quick drying, which makes them tighten up, shrink, and crack.

Secret

When to know your thru-hike may be in jeopardy.

How one goes about their hike is a personal decision. Whether it's to carry three days of food and do big mileage days or carry six days and keep the mileage in the teens is as individual as the decision to hike itself. Some of you will walk every mile with your backpack while some will turn to slack-packing (hiking without your pack) to a location where you get picked up by a hostel shuttle service to address the burden of gear weight or injuries. There's a lot of free time to think about it. Your choices throughout the journey can either keep you emotionally strong or weaken your resolve, and one crack in your armor is often followed by others. Before you know it, your emotional strength can come under constant attack – it's mental pollution that increases your vulnerability. Once again, Hike Your Own Hike. It's your hike and your adventure. I've spoken to those who planned their slack-packing before any tread even touched the trail. As pointed out in Secret #1, Transitioning from Cityness to Wildness, this is a prime example of how Cityness was governing all their pre-hike and early miles on the trail. Concocting ways to ease the effort of a thru-hike before one even starts may seem brilliant, that you're outsmarting the Appalachian mountains, but it's just showing that your mindset may not be ready.

Leaving suburbia and all you know to go on a primitive adventure in the woods requires a bit of passion in your blood, and discussions on how to hike can quickly become controversial. In one breath some will state the Hike Your Own Hike slogan and then chastise you for walking out of a shelter differently than how you walked in. These self-appointed mileage police can be quite opinionated. I sometimes ask them if they walked on both sides of the tree? "Why?" they ask. "Well, if you walked on the wrong side you might have missed part of the AT," I answer.

Even with the best of intentions, there's no guarantee in being christened a Thru-hiker. Georgia to Maine is an enormous distance. So much has to go right. First you need to avoid a hike-ending injury (foot or leg) or other health issues. In '06, the day after crossing the Maine stateline and 1800 miles, I slipped on black ice and did a double somersault that resulted in a broken wrist. Luckily for me, I was able to continue 29 days later with double splints the final three weeks after forcing the doctor to cut off the cast. So some injuries aren't denials, just delays.

Second, family and friends need to stay well – matters on the home-front need to march forward without consequence. So, whether through the avoidance of injury or everything remaining harmonious at home, to actually become a "Thru-hiker" instead of thru-hiking, one needs a bit of luck.

Having a desire to thru-hike doesn't necessarily mean you'll have the resolve. Plenty have stopped in that first 30 miles on the way to the Walasi-Yi Center. Heck, some have stopped on The Approach Trail. For me personally, I feel if you're not having a joyful time then you should by all means get into town and rethink your plan. Life's too precious to trudge rather than hike.

Slack-packing is an attractive enticement, especially when it's promoted by a number of shuttle services to bring in revenue. Slack-packing can be a refreshing change. However, it can in some cases serve as a red flag to your mindset. Taking a few days off to walk without pack weight can be liberating, but many shuttle services will promote how they can drive you to the top of a mountain and let you walk down back to their hostel, then the next day take you back to the top and let you walk down again and on your way. It's a brilliant strategy. This "summit slacking" (my name) gets them two days of shuttle fees plus an overnight fee or two, and you think you've beaten the trail and its difficulty by ingenuity. If that was your goal then I'd say, "Good show, jolly good." However, I'm not sure that finding ways *not to hike* the Appalachian Trail is truly in the spirit of a thru-hike. You rob yourself of how splendidly addictive the toil of an end-to-end journey can be, and at the same time the intensity of pride you'll feel in doing so.

Becoming preoccupied with finding short cuts should be a red flag. I feel it also shows that the adventure isn't completely what you hoped it would be. Consider, as I did once, climbing a bear of an ascent, Three Ridges Mt. in Virginia. As the heat of the day and my mileage total rose, I came to a trail sign announcing a four mile short cut to the shelter, which avoids the long, hot climb over the summit by going left along a side trail rather than continuing straight up the AT's longer 6 mile path. It totally caught me off guard; this would be a test of my integrity. Standing there hot, tired, knowing more heat and fatigue was in my future on the AT, I found a short cut offering me a siren song of choice.

The AT teaches us many things: patience, staying in the moment, and honor. When you succeed and finish the AT, you may submit the achievement to the Appalachian Trail Conservancy, that indeed you have completed all of the mileage of that season's official mileage length. The submission is all based on honor. They, in turn, send you a paper certificate and a small patch of fabric that says, 2000-Miler. The simple designation given to those who claim to have hiked it all. It doesn't matter whether you do it in one year or twenty-one, just that you've done it all – and it's all on the honor system.

Standing there, frozen in the trail, a razor sharp clarity (I suppose this is called an epiphany) offered the simple answer that overpowered my moment of weakness. What occurred to me was the tiny fact that I came to thru-hike the Appalachian Trail not the Mar-Har Trail (short cut). I continued straight, sweat pouring out of me, to a summit that had no vista overlook. These are the moments that can make us waver but inversely help strengthen our mettle.

As stated before, this whole subject matter is quite controversial. Where some feel slack-packing is "Going over to the dark side," I feel you just may need to be on guard a bit if it turns into a practice of avoidance. You may at the moment think you're being clever or brilliant, but the true power is found in not caring what you have to go over or through on a thru-hike. Seeking ways to lessen the trail's difficulty may be actually saying something else, that maybe your gear is too heavy and you should take serious action to rectify it. I once witnessed a self-proclaimed "cheapskate" plop down a thousand dollars for entirely new gear on one town stop. New tent, pack, sleeping bag, stuff sacks, everything, which cut her gear weight by over 20 pounds, with the hope of helping her with her tendonitis – it was a grand display of retail therapy. But alas, the injury would still win in the end and end her hike.

Things happen, and that may be why the phrase, "I'm coming off the trail" rather than "I'm quitting" has become a better expression. These are the things that just happen every season to hikers and why another phrase, "Going too far, too fast, with too much, too soon" is the way some hikers take themselves out of the journey.

In a few locations on the AT, there are alternative routes - official Blue Blazed trails for periods of dangerous weather (lightning) and higher ground routes in times of flooding. These are different than short cuts, designed specifically to keep us safer when conditions merit. For this reason, if you are tenacious enough and joyful enough to reach Maine and the crossing of the Kennebec River, the official way across is by ferry canoe. Painted on the bottom of the canoe's hull is a white blaze, once again to help allow for a safer passage to what can be a less than civilized crossing if the dam upriver has an unannounced water release. Drowning tragedies have happened here.

Slack-packing is not a short cut, a short cut is a short cut and slacking is just another way to make miles with more relaxed shoulders. Slacking is a way to make the AT easier; the AT will never be easy. Some of the AT speed records are basically slack-packing, only they call it "supported" since the "hikers" are more runners carrying nothing – not exactly thru-hiking in the traditional sense with a backpack. Summit slacking makes certain parts of the AT a whole lot easier, but it also prevents you from preparing for the other adversities. There's a lot to be said for the elation from a well-earned climb and hiking memories purely acquired; the example of summit slacking may speak volumes of growing issues inside you. Only you can say.

Yellow blazing is skipping sections altogether by car. (The yellow blazes being the road stripes between lanes.) I offer you a fair warning though, in Bill Bryson's book *A Walk In The Woods*, his yellow blazing skip with sidekick Katz (whether real or fictional) out of frustration in the

Smokys led to destroying their resolve and they failed to complete what was their intended goal of thru-hiking. In my own adventures, one hiker who was putting too much ego into keeping up with some of us, yellow blazed ahead several hundred miles only to have myself and others stroll into a shelter that he was at just a few weeks later. Unable to look any of us in the eye, it was a very uncomfortable, awkward night for him and a long lingering morning as we all moved north with him staying put.

Here's a small nugget of wisdom if you find you're having a crisis moment in your resolve:

"You came to hike the Appalachian Trail rather than find ways not to."

Nobody cares how fast or slow you are. Saying you hiked the entire AT is on the honor system. It is a voluntary endeavor. Either kid yourself or be true to the spirit of a thru-hike with honesty and integrity, it's your choice. Low moments find everyone, it's OK to push the pause button if you're tired of being cold or wet or both. Pausing doesn't mean stopping; regroup in town and continue when you're emotionally recovered. The sun will shine again and moods will rise. Difficulty will fade behind you, while a less than truthful passage will steal your elation, your joy, and your sense of pride. Hike with integrity and by doing so, if you miss a section due to an honest mistake, you'll still sleep well, have an inner peace, and be able to look others in the eye. I know a hiker who fell and destroyed his knee only yards from the famous Mt. Katahdin sign. Racked with pain, he was never able to reach and touch that icon. Never got his Katahdin photo for prosperity. But was still acknowledged by the ATC as a 2000-Miler. I have no issue with that.

There are some colossal AT mountains that can be summit slacked if you have the predisposition, the biggest of these being the monstrous Mt. Washington in New Hampshire or Mt. Greylock in Massachusetts. Summit slacking may be easier on the muscles, but I don't believe it's as beneficial to your emotional strength, the deterioration of which is the main reason someone leaves the trail. In what may be a grand plan of routing, the AT seems to help us teach ourselves different trail mastery in each state. Steep ascents in Georgia, long climbing endurance in North Carolina and Virginia, rock walking and boulder hopping in Pennsylvania and all things boggy in New Jersey and Vermont. We master these, honing our abilities just in time for New Hampshire and Maine where the journey becomes steep, long, rocky, wet and you're wondering if your foot will ever touch flat trail again. Everything there gets ratcheted up to a level of 11 and everything you've learned is utilized.

In regards to mileage short cuts, if I were to guesstimate that every day on the AT you'll walk an extra mile and a half when you factor in blue blaze trails to shelters, water sources, walks to the grocery store, Post Office and such in town, and using a five month hike duration with its plus or minus 150 days, that's roughly 225 miles of additional walking. Seems sort of silly compromising the spirit of an AT thru-hike by skipping sections to avoid miles, doesn't it? Once again, it comes down to your mindset and maybe your joyfulness. Maybe the root of taking short cuts or summit slacking is your lingering cityness impatience controlling you? Clearly an AT thru-hike takes physical stamina and mental/emotional patience; adjusting to the slower pace can be difficult. It's your hike, do so as you wish. It's a wonderful achievement when accomplished honorably.

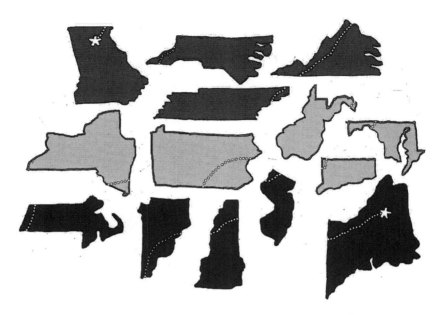

Collect the whole set. Become an AT 2000-Miler.

Secret

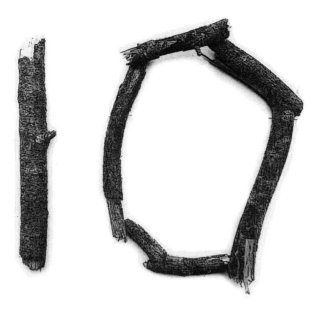

Gear and livability - the balancing act.

Is a backpack that weighs less but is less comfortable worth it? How about a tent that weighs less but is awkward to get in and out of - is that worth it? (Your criteria, your choice obviously.) I suggest you consider the livability (usage and practicality) of your gear in addition to other aspects like their weight – a bold statement coming from someone who hole-punched his Crocs to save a mere ounce!

The gear world and its choices are now vast for light-weight- conscience backpackers, but choosing gear solely for what it weighs can create an unnecessary burden. Since a thru-hike involves a great deal of time living with that gear, your choice can either mean thousands of miles of load-carrying discomfort or gear that is so inconsequential, so unobtrusive that you never give it a thought. Gear should add value to your adventure. Do you really want months of sleeping in inconvenient, cramped quarters or would having a more livable space make more sense? Certainly one can take each philosophy beyond being practical. A larger tent may be easier to live in but the weight could make it far from ideal for a thru-hike. Hence your gear selection will be a balancing act.

There was a time as the lightweight revolution was taking off that designers and enthusiasts lost their focus on products. Unstructured backpacks - packs without frames - started popping up, shamelessly glorifying their incredibly low weight to impress the uninformed. At issue with this is that backpacks are very uncomfortable when the load is literally shouldered by the shoulders and back rather than by the hip belt. When a pack has a frame - a structure to hold it vertical with a hip belt that has some rigidity - 75-80% of the load in that backpack will be carried on the hips where your largest muscles are - your legs and butt. One can hike all day when the load is carried there. Frankly, the structured hip belt might be the single greatest invention to come along in the last hundred years, rivaling sliced bread, indoor plumbing and Post-It Notes - only those aren't particularly important to long-distance backpacking.

These ultra-light, quick-to-market packs were quite uncomfortable and failed to be market successes.

The first criteria in selecting gear you wear is comfort (backpacks, clothes, sleeping bags, etc.) For all the other stuff, stuff that does something (stove, filter, tent, etc.) it should be ease of use, first and foremost. Once they deliver on those basics then weight, compactness, and price should be tiebreakers. In the later sections dedicated to gear choices, I go into this further.

Sleeping bags and starting dates.

It always surprises me how warm we hikers can stay when our packs are tight to our spine, maintaining a good pace and having clothing designed for the endeavor, despite frigid temps. The human motor is an amazing heater. But no matter the start date - early or late - hikers have to stop hiking to rest. That's when the cold can bite with the sharpest of teeth.

It may even happen in July; a weather event roars in and the 80 degree temps of yesterday are just 50 degrees on a ridgeline today. Add wind and rain that will cut right through your thin summer blood and cold ensues. Shivering catches many a hiker off guard since all the winter stuff was mailed home a month ago.

It can actually be warmer to tent out rather than use the shelters on some cold nights. Your 98.6 inside a small tent can make it as much as 10 degrees warmer; you sort of create your own microclimate. As great as the shelter system is on the AT, they can be a frigid place to lay your hat for the night. This is also why it's important to choose properly rated sleeping bags, and sleeping pads with an appropriate R-value.

Since most women sleep colder than men, it's important for them to consider having a woman's specific sleeping bag to get that extra insulation where they need it most - their upper body and feet. I've heard most women carry a 0° to 15° bag, where the men usually carry a 10° to 20° bag when the start date is as early as March 1st (as in "fringe winter," brrr...makes my teeth chatter just thinking about it). Then again, on the AT it could be 60 degrees out. The southern Appalachians weather is nutty that way.

Frankly, if you're beginning in early March I'd err on the warmer rated bag - even a zero degree for both men and women - since temps in the single digits happen regularly. If starting in April, the 15° to 30° range could serve you well, but it all depends of that years winter trend. A cold sleepless night is not something hikers want to repeat. You think you'll just go to sleep and wake in the morning when the sun comes up, but you can't sleep. Your body goes into the fetal position and won't let you fall asleep (defensive act). Pretty much all you can do is shiver and have an awful night. Hikers can always supplement their sleeping bag's warmth with their base layer, jacket, hat, socks, and gloves for added protection.

The ideal would be to have a bag that exceeds the actual temp to be faced. Sort of like how you can drive a Ford Pinto at 85 mph, but it's at the edge of it's performance envelope. Get in a 7-Series BMW and 85 mph doesn't even have it breathing hard (BTW – my old Pinto ended its life in flames, in the mountains, burning out the breaks with me in it. Only just escaped, thankfully with my homework during college.)

Below is my take on temperature needs with a mind-set for facing adversity rather than counting on ideal conditions.

Northbound

March AT start   *Sleeping Bag: EN 0° – 15°*

                        (Plus a liner to extend range)

                        Sleeping Pad R-value: 3.5 or higher

April AT start   *Sleeping Bag: EN 15° – 30°*

                        (Plus a liner to extend range)

                        Sleeping Pad R-value: 2.5 or higher

Southbound

May AT start   *Sleeping Bag: EN 15° – 30°*

                        (Plus a liner to extend range)

Sleeping Pad R-value: 2.5 or higher

The "EN" is an unbiased, truthful temperature rating that stands for European Norm. After years of some sleeping bag manufacturers telling temperature fibs on what their bag performance was (and many a hiker having a cold night), the EN rating system was established in 2005 and uses sensors in mannequins to bring truthfulness to our gear decisions. EN temp ratings factor in that you're wearing base layers top and bottom, hat, gloves and socks to achieve these comfort and lower-limit parameters. The phrase "Comfort" is used to convey what temperature a woman would be comfortable sleeping in. "Lower-Limit" describes what temp a man should be comfortable in. Companies like REI display these ratings on their product cards to add clarity. When EN ratings are posted you'll see unusual temp numbers (17° or 22° or 3°) instead of fudging the numbers by rounding them up or down.

We hikers all have different metabolisms – some hikers get cold easily while some are a raging furnace of heat. It is wise to err on a temp rating for your sleeping bag (within reason) that exceeds what the conditions would most likely be; one can always unzip or pull the hood off the head to cool down. Often in March at elevation, a few days or even a week of single-digit lows are possible. Having a 0° bag or 10° and using your clothes to enhance warmth for such events are erring on the warmer side rather than a bag rated at 20°. I'm not advocating having a 0° bag when a 30° is adequate. Much depends on that year's winter trend and understanding that March and April can have wild swings of the thermometer.

Clothing, as just mentioned, will also supplement your warmth in a pinch. Your camp jacket, fleece hat, dry socks and glove liners can be difference makers at times. However, the wrong clothes inside your bag can leave you colder. When your rain jacket and pants are worn inside your bag, your 98.6 gets trapped, due to the rain gear's infamous lack of breathability. This traps your heat and doesn't let it penetrate into the down or synthetic insulation, which prevents the insulation from lofting up fully. Less loft, less warmth.

Avoid using your rain gear inside your sleeping bag.

A better consideration when needing extra warmth protection would be to zip up your raincoat and pull it over the lower half of your sleeping bag, making it sort like a short bivvy sack for your lower half. Of course you're thinking, "Postcard, why not just put the jacket on over the upper part of you outside your sleeping bag?" Well, if you can actually do that while your arms are inside your bag, you may have a future in Las Vegas opening for Penn & Teller's magic act.

Some hikers, myself included, will opt for having two sleeping bags of different temp ratings (for different periods of time on the trail), while others will try to make do with one and add a liner for the cold start and finish dates. Your progress in miles, along with the natural progression of the season, will determine when your warmer winter bag can be mailed out and replaced if you're opting for two bags.

If you're carrying a 30° bag for an April start, it won't be necessary to switch bags, only I'd carry a liner that adds 15° because a weather event could come sweeping down the plain. Using a liner, early and late in the hiker season can provide a wider temperature protection and can be mailed home during the warmer months. Thirty to 35° is what I recommend (once again, this depends on your pace relative to the season for the end of spring through summer.) My first hike start was April 30th with a 15° down bag, but it got swapped out to my 35° down bag in Hot Springs, NC, just after The Great Smoky Mountains. An older wisdom on the AT is to wait and make the change after you get past Roan Mountain in the Grayson Highlands area of Virginia, which is at 5000 ft of elevation. Once again, it is determined by where you are in the season, your pace, and what that season is like that year.

Weather trends like a cold, lingering winter should take top priority in your decision making rather than past seasons choices made by others. Blindly choosing sleeping bags others have chosen can also be folly if your start dates vary greatly. I know of one hiker who chose the impressive Marmot Helium, a 15° down bag, that she'd read so many others had chosen due to its incredible low weight to warmth rating for her attempt, only she didn't pay attention to when in the season others had used it. So when she started in February instead of April - as many of the reviewers of the bag had - its temp rating was insufficient for the single digit temps. It drove her off the trail and ended that hike.

My second hike start was April 6th with my Marmot Hydrogen 30° bag since it was a warmer winter that year. I do remember having a couple chilly nights at high elevation shelters where my camp jacket helped supplement my sleeping bag's rating. That bag was replaced with my 15° to complete Maine in the month of September after having that 29-day delay from a broken wrist.

After crossing the New Hampshire state line, it would be wise to switch back to the warmer, winter bag (and extra jacket, hat, and gloves) since you're about to enter The Whites. Their higher latitude on the hemisphere, their above-treeline elevation and infamous dramatic weather events require hikers to have all their protection options with them. Due to my pace on my first hike, despite my late May 1st start, I entered The Whites and The Bigelow mountains of Maine in the middle of August. My 35 ° Western Mountaineering down bag by that time wasn't delivering the rating from all the time in it – definitely could have used a laundering and a reloft. I had some chilly nights as a result; a liner would have helped. Typically this warmer gear (clothes and sleeping bag) will be kept for the rest of the journey to the northern terminus, Mt. Katahdin.

A note on laundering your down sleeping bag (or jacket for that matter): Down feathers have natural oils that react to our body heat, causing them to loft up, delivering insulation and warmth. Those oils need to remain on the feathers, so some extra care in washing needs to take place. Unlike Tide or Era or any normal detergents that remove our body oils from our suburban clothes, Down Wash by Nikwax retains the oils on the feathers. Remove the down oils while cleaning in normal detergent and your bag will no longer be rated to the same temp. Your down bag should be washed in a front loader only and never a top loader with the center agitator, which can tear the baffles that hold feathers in compartments to keep your bags warmth uniform throughout. After the wash, dry the down bag on delicate heat for two or three cycles with a clean tennis ball tossed in. This helps to prevent the feathers from clumping, which could cause a loss of loft.

After each outing, consider unzipping your sleeping bag to sit outside in the sunshine and fresh air for the day before storing it in its larger storage bag. This small ritual will reduce the need to wash it. Additionally, most bags are fine to sleep in 20 to 30 times before needing a wash, and only then if the bag smells. A synthetic bag's insulation doesn't require a special washing agent, but I'd follow the same airing out rituals just listed. If you have a synthetic insulation sleeping bag, another Nikwax water-based product called Tech Wash can help remove lingering odors.

Your sleeping bag is the one place where you can retreat to for physical recovery and warmth. But more importantly, it's where you retreat for your emotional recovery as well. As a result, my council is to not skimp on the quality of your bag or bags. Since down is an organic insulation, it is quite hardy and will outlast synthetic insulation; your investment will have greater longevity. Although it's true that a synthetic bag can still deliver some warmth if wet, it won't deliver its full rating. I'd counter by saying no one I know wants to slide into a wet bag of any kind. So whether you go with synthetic or down, acquire an ultra-sil, lightweight, waterproof dry bag of about 20-liters to drop it into. Simply use the stuff sack or compression sack your bag comes with and then drop that into the dry sack – squeeze the air out and then roll the top down three times and buckle. Even if it rains an inch an hour and the cats-and-dogs deluge is joined by water buffalo and hippos, you'll arrive in camp with a toasty, dry sleeping bag, thus eliminating the argument of avoiding down. Down is the lightest weight, most compressible relative to warmth insulation, and it's my recommendation for an AT thru-hike.

In 2004, The Weather Channel reported that due to three hurricane remnants moving up the East coast, my first thru-hike year was the fifth wettest on record. By following the technique just outlined, I never arrived at my end of day location with a wet down bag. Oh sure, I might have been wetter than a Bonito in the Bahamas, my sleeping bag wasn't.

Another consideration to point out in the selection process is the sleeping bag's livability. Some of you hikers are the size of a football player. You're tall and have shoulders and chests that rival a refrigerator. Long and wide options allow male and female hikers a night's sleep without feeling straight-jacketed. Bigger women needing more space can choose one of the longer, wider men's bags, only you might have to go to a rating warmer than you think.

It is important to note that there is a disparity in insulation needs between men's and women's bags. Example – The North Face, synthetic Cat's Meow for men was once rated at 23°. The same Cat's Meow for women was 34° since no extra insulation had been added to where women needed it most - the upper body and footbox areas. All they did was make it shorter.

That 11-degree disparity that once existed on the Cat's Meow is not isolated. The REI Igneo down bag is 19° for men, but 30° for a woman. Many a time women show up after a cold night in their husband's or boyfriend's sleeping bag to buy a new bag. Don't blame the men ladies; most men don't know of the temp disparity. Honest mistakes happen. If it says "unisex", it means it is patterned off of men's temp ratings, not women's.

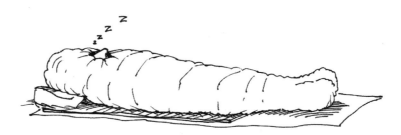

Other than my nose, you're looking at my Tyvek shelter sheet (30" X 7 ft), my Therm-a-rest Z Lite pad (just 6 panels) and my clothes bag "pillow".

Other candidates for these wider bags are those who simply get a bit anxious from the slim dimensions of a normal mummy. Claustrophobic triggers vary from person to person. For some it's the hood, others it's the footbox or arm space. Wider bags may be heavier, but they provide a solution to get you out into adventure. Even hikers who are not officially claustrophobic can have a period of acclimation to a mummy bag. I went from a few anxious moments early on to having only my nose poking out on occasion. You will acclimate and as the days become weeks, you'll come to down right cherish the simplicity and performance of your sleeping bag.

Sleeping bag specs.

Here are the length designations.

Men's "Regular" is for: Anyone 6 feet tall or shorter

Men's "Long" is for: 6 feet 6 inches tall or shorter

Women's "Regular" is for: 5 feet 6 inches tall or shorter

Women's "Long" is for: 6 feet tall or shorter

Caveat: I'm 5 ft 12 inches (just seeing if you're paying attention), better known as 6 ft tall. My 35° Western Mountaineering bag listed itself for those 5 ft 10 inches, and yet I was able to use it. A bit tight at first, but gracious, it only weighed one pound.

Another option for consideration is some men have chosen a woman's bag for length appropriateness rather than the six foot men's "Regular". When they do that they get a much warmer bag than the woman's rating. The women's Marmot Ouray is 3°, but if a man uses it the rating would be -12° (a crazy 15° more warmth). Although a man gains in warmth, he loses in shoulder dimensions. Only the slimmest of men will get their shoulders comfortably in a woman's bag since most women's bags have a different shape. The shoulder/hip space is close to identical in a woman's bag where the widest dimension in a men's bag is the shoulder-chest measurement.

Another common practice of those who absolutely detest slipping on one's frosty hiking clothes on a mountain's low morning temps is to opt for a long bag where you'll have space beyond your feet to stow your clothes for a toasty morning put-on. (Hey, whatever works.) Some of my most courageous moments were from sucking it up for the frosty clothes dressing in the morning. One morning was so cold the hiking shirt was frozen stiff! Awful events (in my alter-ego, Cupcake sort of way) like these eventually forced me to change my choreography of dressing. Unless my hiker clothes are wet, I wear them to bed. By closing my long pant around my ankles and then pulling my socks over the bottom cuffs, the pants don't ride up my legs when I slip into the bag. This added to my toasty twilight slumber, but it was a practice I didn't adopt until my second thru-hike. This small adjustment eliminated the Antarctic clothing moment. A side benefit to sleeping in one's hiking clothes was how it led to quicker morning starts. Often, I could wake, have my breakfast milkshake, pack and be gone before others had their frosty pants on. I became the grand master of the quick start!

Sleeping pads and the cccold.

Conduction is the transfer (or stealing) of heat from a small object to a larger object. Since you and I are smaller than the Earth, it makes us colder if we lie in our sleeping bags without something between the ground and us. That is where sleeping pads come to the rescue. Without a pad between the ground and us our EN bag rating will not be achieved – their testing is done with an insulated pad. With a pad, your bag will deliver a toasty night of deep REM.

Whether the pads are closed cell foam, self-inflating air mattresses or manual blow up air pads, all will have an insulating merit grade, called an R-Value. An R-Value allows you to judge each pad's insulation protection. Although everyone gets cold to different degrees, I try to advise others that if you're going out in the winter, an R-Value of 4.0 or higher would do its job in helping you have a cozy warm sleep. Other charts I've seen recommend an R-Value of 5.0 or higher for winter camping. If only a summer camper, you can accept the most meager of ratings, say 1.0 or better. For both my thru-hikes I used the Therm-a-Rest Z Lite closed cell foam pad. At 6 feet in length with 14 accordion panels from the factory, if one has a mind to (and a knife), one can customize said pad to 6 panels - just enough cushioning and insulation from shoulder blades to butt. (If one were, say...6 feet tall.) This is all I've needed to have a good rest during the months of the journey. Since my head is in the sleeping bag hood and my clothes bag (with some strategic restuffing) transforms into a pillow that rests between the bag's hood and the ground, having a pad there was not needed. FYI – you don't put a pillow inside the bag's hood. Instead, keep the hoods insulation close to your head for max warmth, with the pillow (clothes bag masquerading as actual camp pillow) resting out-side and underneath the hood. See earlier illustration.

This shortened pad length would not provide much in the way of insulation if I were to start in February or early March, when the odds of southern Appalachian snows and single digit temps are likely. But that has never been my plan. The AT is tough enough without snow, and the season is long enough that starting in April can still pro-vide time to spare. My intention was to save weight and pack volume without imposing hardship. After months on the trail, I found this Mini-Me version of a pad to be truly luxurious at night. My, how the trail changes us.

Pads can slip out from underneath your bag through the night if you are a tosser-and-turner. To combat this, many pads are now designed with thicker edges or inflatable rails running the length of the pad. This helps to valley your body to the middle, so you stay centered during a high-energy dream of devouring a double-choc-olate cake. If your pad doesn't have the new design, you can use the old trick of small dollops or smears of clear silicone in random patches along the pad. These act as tiny grippers to your sleeping bag's slippery surface. (Many a time during my hikes I'd wake in the morning half on, half off my meager pad due to my fidgety sleeping - another reason why I took Tylenol PM each night during my thru-hikes.)

If you're a side sleeper, which means more body weight spread over less pad area, you may want to consider inflatable pads with a "quilting" layout rather than length-wise long air rail designs. You'll sink less into the quilt designs like the Big Agnes Q-Core pads than, say, an REI Stratus pad. (Just a thought).

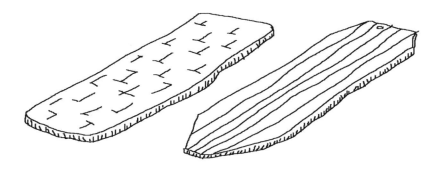

Quilted air pad design and length-wise air chamber design.

Sleeping Bag Liners.

Compact and lightweight, a liner is about giving you options. They can keep your sleeping bag cleaner inside, even fresher in regards to odor and add warmth or wicking properties in hot and cold climates depending on their material. Liners can add an additional 8 °, 14°, 20°

or even 25° of extra warmth to your sleeping bag temp rating. If you fret the cold, carry one. It's better to have it and not use it than to need it blah blah blah. Sorry for the cliché. It's always better to avoid facing a cold, longgg night from a bag with insufficient temp protection.

Using some of the warm climate liners (Coolmax) can serve to wick sweat and assist in cooling and keeping the thru-hiker smell from penetrating into your sleeping bag's fabric. In town you can throw any of the liners in with your clothes during laundry (along with your stuff sacks) to keep your passage a bit more civilized and odor controlled.

The easiest way to use one is to simply step into the liner and then get in your sleeping bag. Voila! Your liner is in your bag and, even if a visit to the woods at 2am is needed, the liner will pretty much stay put in the bag. When the season's temps rise, just send it home during a town stop.

Liners – They come rectangle and mummy. They even come as doubles. They can add warmth or coolness. They can be an add-on or a stand-alone. They give you options.

It all starts with the Backpack.

You can't very well backpack from Georgia to Maine if you don't have a backpack, now, can you? So what should you get? How big does it need to be?

One of the shortest measurements of time known to science is the time between the decision to thru-hike to the time you run down to buy your new backpack. Surpassed only by the amount of time from when the light turns green and someone behind you honks.

It truly is a giddy time when you have clarity of mission and it's time to go buy all the gear toys. I think we can all agree that there are so many wonderful doodads and whiz-bangs one can acquire. Surely a candle lantern in my tent will help me find coziness in the wild! A stainless steel multi-tool that has so many tool options one can build a small house must be a necessity, right?

When it comes to choosing a backpack, the choices are vast. The majority found today are internal frame packs. These are packs where the structure (frame) is hidden from sight underneath the fabric. They are slender in width, keeping them inside your shoulders, thus making them nimble and maneuverable in more rugged terrain. Internal frame backpacks wrap themselves around the wearer like fingers around an apple. This also allows you to feel one with the pack by having it aligned closely to your natural center of gravity. You might also think of internal frame packs as those where everything goes inside, for the most part.

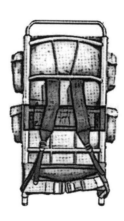

External Frame, from days of old.

Internal Frame Backpacks, from more modern thinking.

The older style of backpack that has the frame outside the fabric bag is called an external frame pack. External frame packs can trace their history back a hundred years to the old pack board, where everything got tied on and then laboriously hauled on the shoulders and achin' back. Yikes. I'm just spit-balling this, but someone back then probably got tired of trying to untie all those darn knots and finally said, "Hey, let's stick a bag on this board," and the external frame pack was born. Or something like that. Anyway, their limited bag size can't hold everything inside, so much of the equipment gets lashed to the exterior frame, which means more knots. The frame usually is wider, closer to your shoulder width. The frame is usually composed of straight tubes with no contours to follow your body or bring loads closer to your center of gravity. Straps, when tightened, just pressed the frame to the body. A few modern internal design comfort revelations have been added to the external frame pack, but few models still exist today.

A simple look at multi-day backpacks at REI might count 160 internal frame choices and just 3 or 4 external. Maybe what that means is that hikers prefer the load-carrying comfort and better balance of the internal design. It's not that external packs don't work, it's just that the Smithsonian wants all its exhibits back. A typewriter can produce a wonderful letter; our word processing software and computer can do it with aplomb.

This is where I quote, again, there's no one-way to go backpacking. Go heavy. Go light. Go old school or new. Just go.

Pack Size.

Backpacks today have two measurements. The first measurement is a number in the name of the pack. Where once manufacturers would name their packs heroic names like Soaring Eagle or Grand Canyon, which did little to tell the buyer what they were buying. Now, thank goodness, common sense naming has won the day. Packs now have names such as Flash 65 or Traverse 85 or Ariel 55 - the number tells us the capacity of the pack in liters. By adding the number, we all now know quickly what the pack can carry in volume.

The second measurement on packs is the size that would best fit our torso. Torso size is the length from the top of your hip bone - known as your iliac crest - to your C7 vertebrae at the base of your neck.

Your C7 vertebrae is easy to find, just stand straight and tall and then only bend at your neck to look at your shoes. There, poking out on your shoulder line arch, just at the base of your neck, is your other landmark for measuring.

Now that you have the two points of your anatomy, what is the distance in inches? That number will determine your torso size. Although there are some variances, for the most part 15-16 inches is a size Extra-Small, 16-17 inches is a Small, 18-19 is a Medium, 20-21 a Large and 22 and up an Extra-Large. When between two sizes like 19 1/2 inches, pick the smaller of the two choices. In this case, get a medium rather than the large to make sure the shoulder straps wrap over the shoulder and touch your upper back. When a pack is too tall, the shoulder straps exit off the top of your shoulder and join the pack without ever touching the back side of the shoulder. This results in the pack just pressing against you rather than wrapping around you. Having the pack wrap around your torso tends to be much more comfortable. More importantly though, is having the proper size shoulder harness to provide your neck with more space. The narrowest part of the shoulder strap harness is where it meets the pack itself. If the pack is too tall for your torso, that narrowest part will be right at your neck as it moves over your shoulders. Not good. Get measured and get the pack that fits your torso.

With a simple change to your approach when putting on a pack, your odds that all will be comfortable increase. Before lifting your pack, loosen all the straps that are to be tightened - Hipbelt, Shoulder Straps, Load Lifters (the little straps above the shoulder straps), Load Stabilizers (the little ones on the side of the hipbelt) and Sternum Strap (the one between the shoulder straps). Only put the pack on once all the straps are loosened (what I refer to as being "neutral"). When the straps are then tightened in the proper order, your pack will customize itself to your anatomy.

Additionally, if you can adjust your habit from just undoing the buckles to take your pack off to one where you loosen all the straps first before unbuckling, then when the pack comes off for breaks it will be sitting there with all the straps neutral, ready to be put back on when break time is over. Just lift and tighten in the proper order to find that custom, comfortable fit again and again for 2000 miles. Adapting this habit is just a tad more efficient. Since you'll take your pack on and off an estimated 7 times a day, that means being more efficient with your pack straps nearly 1000 times in the journey.

No matter how long one has backpacked in their life, I constantly meet some who never learned how strap tightening in a better order can result in more comfortable miles.

#3 - Load Lifters (pull forward to align pack weight with your spine. This is the "that feels better" strap.

#5 - Sternum Strap (many have a whistle on them for emergencies, which if blown 3 times means someone needs help).

#2 - Shoulder Straps (tighten by pulling back rather than straight down).

#1 - Hip Belt (tighter than any belt you'll ever use for your pants).

#4 - Load Stabilizers (not all packs have them).

The proper order for tightening straps can be remembered as Big to Small. So the ideal order for tightening the pack is, hip belt, shoulder straps, load lifters, load stabilizers and finally the sternum strap. By starting with the bottom, the hip belt, it becomes the foundation on which your pack weight sits and the upper straps become secondary.

Maybe understanding where backpacks are carried will help with the whole strap tightening thingy. Despite the name "back" pack, the pack's weight is carried on the hips thanks to the hip belt. When worn tighter than any belt to hold up your pants, the hip belt will carry 75 to 80% of the pack weight (by my guess-timation). This is where your biggest, strongest muscles in your body are located - your legs and butt. When the hip belt isn't worn tight to the hips, the load weight will droop onto your shoulders and neck, and no one I know wants to carry 30 or more pounds on their achin' shoulders and back for 20 miles per day. If all is adjusted well, the load lifter origin on each shoulder strap - called the Point Of Origin – should be at the top middle of your shoulder. A visit to REI can get you finessed if needed. Try to place the hip belt buckle about three fingers below your belly-button for proper location.

To take the pack off, reverse the pack tightening order, sort of. I usually leave my shoulder straps for last and then grab that small handle strap at the top/back of the pack called the "haul loop". The haul loop is designed to lift the weight of the pack, not the more typical bad habit of lifting it by one of the shoulder straps. One shoulder strap is not designed for lifting - doing so can tear the stitching and shorten your pack's longevity.

Whining that it's too complicated or fussy to remember the order? Well, what *isn't* complicated or fussy when learning anything new? You don't get the dance steps correct the first time you try either; you'll know it by heart after a half-dozen times and then the remaining thousand lifts on a thru-hike will be a snap.

Hikers can go all day with their loads when the weight is carried on their hips, but can barely make it a mile without whining when it's on their back and shoulders. So, wear your hip belt tighter than any belt for your trousers and wear your upper straps – your shoulder, sternum and load lifters – just firmly enough to feel them. Let comfort rule the day. This will result in broader smiles and you being more pleasant to be around. Always a good thing.

Where the hip belt is worn follows two schools of thought. Since we measure using the top of the hip bone - the iliac crest - many feel that's where it is carried. Unfortunately, that means the hip belt will be on top of your stomach and it's not called a stomach belt. Because our breathing pump is a result of our diaphragm, squeezing our stomach this way complicates our ability to breathe on those Georgia-to-Maine climbs. The other school of thought happens to be the guidelines that our American military service men and women follow. The hip belt goes on the hips, and the body landmark that helps with its placement is buckling your hip belt buckle about two inches below your bellybutton – three fingers is a quick distance measure. If you don't have a bellybutton then it's a bit more difficult.

Remember though, once you tighten your upper straps to a level of comfort, or any strap for that matter, they're placement is not fixed. They can be tweaked, loosened, tightened. As your under-the-skin fluids adjust to the straps intrusion, straps that started tight can become loose as the fluids relocate. Your straps' adjustment is a fluid situation. After my straps initial tightening followed by a slight tweak ten or so minutes later, I would routinely hike for three hours without ever touching them again.

What size pack for a thru-hike?

Now that you know how to wear your pack, what capacity does one need for a thru-hike? You know that old expression of the "tail wagging the dog"? Choosing what size capacity of pack is sort of like that. A pack is a vessel to carry your stuff, so certainly a good question to ask is, "What is the size of your stuff?" It obviously makes little sense buying a 50-liter pack when you're carrying a synthetic sleeping bag rated for zero-degrees or having a full size, two person tent – items that commonly are of larger volume.

However, if your sleeping bag is made of down and you carry a one-person, backpackers tent or hammock, then a 50-liter pack could be appropriate; a backpack of 45 liters (ultralighters) to 65 liters could be ideal for a thru-hike of the AT.

This range allows for the bulkier cold weather clothing early on yet it's not so large that its volume is a hindrance in the warmer months when less clothing is required. Your start date determines much of your clothing needs as well as your hiker profile, whether you're an ultralighter, willing to do without certain amenities or if you're a take-everything backpacker.

One hiker during my 2006 thru-hike only carried 17 pounds with food and water. Only he didn't have all the appropriate clothing to keep oneself protected from what the AT can toss at you, nor did he have gear that offers hiking options such as having a full-size headlamp. Neither of us had a second insulated jacket we could sweat into. That forced me off a Smokys ridgeline in that hypothermic moment that was addressed in clothing. His only light source was a Princeton Tec Pulsar finger light. That light source really won't allow you to see the trail if you need to move in darkness before sunrise or a late arrival; hey, things happen. One morning on a very early start hours before sunrise, he had to walk behind me for two hours to see where the trail was. (A position that his long legs and quick pace were unfamiliar with.) His light source was adequate for around camp or shelter, but not for much else. (For the record, the tiny Pulsar light is my backup light if my spare batteries or headlamp both were to fail.) But ultralighters put weight as the most important criteria and have no issue sacrificing on livability or practicality.

On the flip side are those hikers who carry every amenity they can ponder like a full bar for cocktails, Belgian waffle irons, food for two weeks, chairs and thick novels with flickering candle lanterns for cozy ambiance. Their backpacks are more in the range of 70, 80, even 100-liters for vast amounts of wilderness conquering options. (Just kidding on the waffle iron - keeping you on your toes.)

While working at REI, I do meet male hikers who take pride in how much they can carry. They feel that lugging around heavier loads is something positive, something honorable, I suppose? Certainly on an adventure to Alaska where resupply is a bit more challenging, these larger capacity packs are not a choice but an essential. On the AT, though, resupply can happen every 3 to 6 days in most cases. Not comprehending the composition of the AT contributes to many of the heavier thru-hiking pack weights at the start. This might be because of a lack of knowledge or using gear that is older or already owned, which tends to be bulkier and heavier. Or maybe they're unwilling to make the hard choices to reduce the items taken. Hikers will routinely pare down gear and mail it home or drop it into a hiker box (a freebie box of stuff for any hiker who wants it).

Hikers who hesitated to make decisions on gear before the first step taken will liberally shed items without pause when they discover gravity and mountains are not friends. Changing to lighter, smaller, more joyful options despite the money also leads to lighter, smaller, more joyful backpacks.

I have had the unfortunate experience of carrying a 102-liter backpack with a horrific 54-pound load simply because I didn't know any other way. Early in my hiking acclimation, those miles proved to be a powerful teaching moment. When the weather turned damp and all the fabrics in my load gained moisture weight, my teaching moment heightened the urgency to find a smarter way.

The common mistake here is that anything as gargantuan as a 2000-mile hike for half a year must need the biggest, baddest backpack an outfitter might sell. Since I didn't know better and walked into a store where the staff had zero knowledge of thru-hiking, I left with a behemoth of a pack that wasn't even the correct torso size, but I was as giddy as a child that I had my new toy for adventure. As I revealed in my first book and at my Outdoor School classes, the reason I bought my 102-liter backpack was because it was ...blue.

Not everyone thinks that a big pack is overkill as I would come to understand, which was the case of a trail friend I met during my first thru-hike.

Coming around a bend at the summit of an early climb, now carrying my smart-ish load of 30 pounds and striding well without need of a summit rest, there on the ground, face beet red with exhaustion, was Carp. Catching his breath and composure, we made introductions and started a leap frog friendship. Now, Carp was much tougher than myself.

After retiring from ten years in Australia's Special Forces, Carp decided to bring his 80lb pack to the relentless ups and downs of the southern Appalachians. Carp's 120+ liter backpack and his 80lb load tied for the largest I've witnessed on the AT in my 5000 miles. A bit of a result of his military "what if" conditioning – Carp's load included a one pound gun shot wound first aid kit and a two-person, heavy mountaineering tent. Upon reaching the outfitter at Neels Gap, Carp boldly (albeit hesitantly) whittled 20 lbs out to mail home.

It's important to note here that pack size and weight won't determine whether you achieve Thru-hiker status; going light merely increases your odds. Carp made it all the way with 60lbs while others carrying 25 did not.

My hiking approach could now be classified as a Luxury Lightweighter. I do dabble in ultra-light nuttiness, but I also want to have options with clothing protection and traditional tents over bare-minimum tarps. Under the philosophy of lightweight backpacking, you have everything you need and only a few things you want. The classification of luxury lightweighter meant being prepared for many situations, but not necessarily using the lightest products the gear world had to offer.

The backpack that started with me on my first thru-hike was a rushed to market "ultra-lightweight" pack from the people famous for making heavy, expedition-size tanks: Gregory. Apparently, feeling the gear world and the lightweight gear revolution was passing them by Gregory introduced the G-Pack at 48-liters of ultra-sil nylon. This sub 3 lb pack apparently made it to market without the appropriate R&D testing. Unable to carry my 33 pounds, both shoulder straps ripped out of the pack body 100 miles into the journey, leaving me without working shoulder straps! Forced to "MacGyver" a solution with Velcro straps, I turned my hipbelt into a stomach belt and used the sternum strap to create a cage around my chest – an unpleasant but manageable fix to the next outfitter 80 miles away. My pack's self-destruction wasn't isolated and happened to many who opted for this dazzling, new lightweight pack from the respected maker.

Upon reaching the NOC - the Nantahala Outdoor Center - I bought its new big brother - the Gregory Z-Pack at 55 liters-to handle my 33 pounds. Before I reached Pearisburg, Virginia, the shoulder straps ripped out once again, forcing another hundred miles of gear McGyvering. Two major market failures and two major black marks to a once beyond reproach reputation.

Well, fool me once, shame on you. Fool me twice, shame on me. With that I called the wonderful Mt. Rogers Outfitters on Main Street in Damascus, Virginia and bought a pack made by a small garage business in Utah. Well known in thru-hiker circles, ULA's (Ultra Lightweight Adventure) 50-liter, P2 backpack became my companion for the rest of the adventure. At just two pounds five ounces, it made it all the way to Mt. Katahdin and then again on the entire length of my second AT thru-hike without consequence. Always a good thing. Today, ULA is no longer owned by its creator, but they still make good packs. The P2 was replaced years ago with the Catalyst – it's their workhorse and ideal for thru-hikes.

Although 45- to 65-liter backpacks can work, you need to factor in your load weight as well. Ultralight packs have their limits, and the AT is a tough place and things happen. The previous examples touched more on poor quality and design. It doesn't necessarily mean that lightweight packs can't carry 35 pounds well. But when loads start reaching 35 pounds plus, these lightweight packs' longevity can be compromised. Wearing it can feel unruly, sort of like all the padding on the shoulder straps is getting crushed, offering little comfort.

My first thru-hike pack weight was 33 pounds with five days of food and 2-liters of water on an April 30th start up The Approach Trail. With a start date that late, once I got past the Smokys, I switched out my 15-degree bag for my 35 and sent home some extra clothes, resulting in a 2 lb weight savings. When I acquired the ULA pack I dropped an additional two pounds. My resupply, first-day-back-out load remained around 29 pounds all the way to Maine, and always lightened up by about 1.5 pounds each day due to consumed food weight. Darn good.

As my knowledge grew, my pack weight shrank. On that wonderful, sunny April 6th morning I started up the

Approach Trail to begin my second thru-hike, the same ULA P2 load came in at 27 pounds with five days of food and two liters of water at morning start – five days was routinely my load.

Today's ultralight backpacks still have their limitations. What may be comfortable to wear with 25 lb loads can quickly become uncomfortable with 35 lbs. If hip belts aren't stable enough or the density of the shoulder strap foam is too flimsy, the hiker will not be happy. The pack should match the load. If you are unable or unwilling to upgrade to lighter gear, then chose a heavier pack with more robust qualities to better handle the load weight.

Wonderfully, ultralight packs with good, comfortable structures are now numerous. Packs in the 2 to mid-3 pound range give thru-hikers options. I would even consider a pack in the 4-pound range that was ultra comfortable like the Osprey Aether 60. Only I'd remove the pack's floating lid, and use just the main body of the pack. This minimizes strap buckling and unbuckling during the duration of the hike. With that in mind, Osprey's Exos 58 is ideal for thru-hiking since they added a fabric flap on the top of the main body to use if the floating lid is removed – a smart option. A size medium would then weigh in at around 2 pounds 3 ounces and has good structure to carry loads in the 30 lbs or less range.

Located on the sternum strap of many backpacks today is a whistle-buckle. The use of a whistle is the universal call for help. In the case of an emergency or injury where you cannot self-evacuate, the human voice wouldn't have the decibel level nor the endurance to keep yelling for help. Three blasts of a whistle tells others that someone is needing help. So, remember: three blasts, just in case. If your pack doesn't have a sternum whistle, then get a whistle of some type to have. It is one of the Ten Essentials of the backcountry.

Considerations for a tent.

Despite watching our weight on gear, do not choose anything simply because it's the lightest. Yes, this is a bold statement coming from someone who hole punched his Crocs to save an ounce, isn't it? That is why I'm even more qualified to offer common sense about gearing up.

Your gear criteria should place as much importance on comfort, livability or ease of use as it does on being lightweight.

One day at REI I met a young, savvy man who was asking tent weight questions. He was literally creating an Excel spread sheet of all the lightest weight gear options to determine what he should acquire before he pulled out his wallet. (No really, an Excel spread sheet. Any of you do that?)

"OK, great, but that might not be in your best interest," I said to Mr. Excel, triggering a raised eyebrow. To him, gear that weighed the least was gear that was the best.

He was focusing simply on the weight of the tent. It can be a bit misleading since phrases like "Minimum Weight" are often confused with being all that you need. Minimum Weight is the tent, rainfly and poles. No footprint (ground sheet), no stakes or guylines to anchor it, and no stuff sacks to organize it all. Then there's "Trail Weight" or "Fast Pitch Weight", which is only the fly, footprint and poles. This combo omits the tent body with its waterproof, bathtub floor and its full bug protection, which is why most buy a tent. Go figure!? Ultralight backpackers are willing to forgo these "luxuries" to achieve load lightness goals. "Packaged Weight" is the entire tent as you slide it off the store shelf. Remember, there's no one way to go backpacking - you make decisions on areas that are important to your sensibilities. Me, I don't want creepy crawlies joining me in my sleeping bag and I simply detest that buzzing of mosquitos around my ears at night when I want to sleep. I want my tent sleeping to include the tent. Call me crazy.

When judging weights between choices, make sure it's Packaged Weight to Packaged Weight, apples to apples. You can easily make a wrong purchase if you're comparing packaged weight apples to trail weight oranges, as the saying sort of goes.

The lightweight gear revolution has spread to all areas of gear. Choices in single-person tents that were limited to a few 4 lb options have now been replaced by vast choices tipping the scale at 3 and even 2 pounds. Tarps have always offered sub-2 lb options, as long as you're willing to relax your requirements for critter control (creepy crawlers, mosquitos, ticks, tarantulas, Burmese Pythons, gila monsters and amorous field mice). There's also the annoyance of not having residual splash up protection from a hard rain with tarps.

"Hey Norbert, interested in a burrito?"

"I do love those gooey centers."

Today there's a dearth of lightweight tents that sacrifice nothing in protection, but unfortunately don't always provide their dwellers with optimum livability. Many of the lightest tents have a door on the front of the tent, requiring the occupant to crawl in or out on all fours. Not too big a deal, unless you hike on the eastern corridor of the United States that is known for being infamously wet. Crawling out to the wet that is the AT and then crawling back in from the wet leaves something to be desired. Additionally, having no shoulder width or decent peak height to allow you to sit up, well... something as simple as sitting up inside a nylon structure can feel so civilized.

Practically speaking, long-distance hiking tends to leave one's leg muscles a bit tight. Whether it's those early weeks when leg muscles are being tested or in later months when your miles ramp up, leg stretches can help keep late night leg cramps at bay. Stretching my legs before bed became a nightly routine on both of my thru-hikes.

You'd be hard-pressed to do a Yoga Seated Forward Bend (Paschimottanasana) or a Left/Right Twist (Marichyasana) in some of those minimal shelters that lack shoulder space or good peak height. So long as your only desire is to crawl in, limit your activities to guidebook reading, journaling, and catching Z's, and you have no issue with a smaller vestibule, some of these tents can be great for weight savings.

Consider this, however: if you want a more effortless entry/exit, then go for a single-person tent with a side door. This makes for an easier in-and-out since you can be on your knees inside the tent and step up to you feet with a single side step. No mud crawling. A tent design that widens at the shoulder end but narrows at the foot end provides a higher degree of livability inside without excessive weight added on. Wed that to a peak height that allows you to sit up and have shoulder space so you can get dressed or do modest leg stretches. All this can add value to your tent for the long journey. It's those small comforts that may appear trivial at first that prove their worth over many months, thus assisting with your emotional strength.

Additionally, there are benefits to having a freestanding or semi-freestanding tent, especially when you get to The White Mountains of New Hampshire. A freestanding tent means a tent that stands erect without having to be staked out. It usually has grommet holes on fabric wings at each corner for the poles to slip into. A semi-free-standing tent might use your hiking poles in some con-figuration or just needs a limited number of stakes to reach its full shape. The use of your hiking poles is com-mon in ultra-light tents, mostly to achieve height, but I have one – the Tarptent Rainbow - where poles are used laying down at the ends to make the base. Freestanding design helps in The Whites where tents must be set up on wooden platforms.

*Four 1-person tents crammed onto one tent platform
in The Whites of New Hampshire.*

Faced with these livability particulars, our Mr. Excel Spread Sheet said he'd need to reassess his criteria.

Hammocks are popular, but one needs the disposition and makeup for one. If you're a sound sleeper, not a tosser/turner, then a hammock might be an option, but stomach sleepers might not be as happy. My hammock-sleeping trail friends were so passionately in love with them that several set them up in the backyard and continued to use them after being home. One set it up in his bedroom and left the linens on the bed unwrinkled for ages.

In summary, design aspects to consider:

· *A tent with a side door for easier entry/exit.*
· *Tents that offer shoulder width when sitting up.*

- *Tents that have good peak height, 37" or higher.*
- *Packaged weight vs. other packaged weight comparisons.*
- *Freestanding or semi-freestanding.*

No matter your choice, set it up in the backyard or living room and be proactive with seam sealing. Get some clear silicone and some mineral spirits. In a cup, mix a 50/50 mixture of the two and stir them together. The thick, goopy silicone will breakdown into an easy paint on gel. A nice half-inch brush will cover all your rainfly seams and floor seams without excessive weight. Take time to do this before you leave so you can have fewer surprises in the wilderness. For you neat nicks, one can cut a half-inch wide slot in a piece of cardstock about 8 inches long. It becomes a template that makes that entire seam sealing a thing of beauty. Just paint on the sealer, letting the template keep it all uniform.

Plan for adversity and celebrate the ideal rather than plan for the ideal and face the adversity. I suppose that's another Postcard-ism.

Now you're cookin'.

There's nothing like a hot dinner after a day of rain, cold or long miles. As I previously pointed out in "Secret 3: Eat Happy Hike Happy," your abnormal environment of the Appalachian Mountains will be a touch more normal when you're truly enjoying your food. A hot, feel-good-inside dinner can bring tranquility to your spirit, lessen the less-than-ideal day or be the cherry on top of a stupendous one. Hot chocolate and fancy cookies will serve as your culinary crescendo.

The thru-hiker way to a hot meal is wide and varied. Here we'll discuss alcohol and solid fuel tab stoves (the lightest), canister, liquid fuel, and wood burning options as well. We'll also discuss going cold – no hot meals at all.

Historically, when pack weights hovered above the 40 pound range, the good ol' MSR Whisperlite (and like-minded liquid fuel versions) was the standard path to a hot meal. Its compact folding stove legs, large pot platform and multiple sized fuel bottle options provided the thru-hikes with choices. These portable kitchens were valued then and now for their cold weather and high elevation performance, but this came at a price: nearly a 2 pound one. Additionally, if you over primed the fuel cup - the stage that preheats a brass tube to turn liquid fuel to gas vapor - the easily overflowing fuel turned into table fires, shelter floor fires and all nature of fire-induced panic.

Early in my enthusiastic acclimation to this backpacking thingy, and wanting to demonstrate my newly acquired wilderness mojo to a friend, I indeed started a floor fire. Only mine was in my loft on the hardwood living room floor. Calmly, to my credit, I lifted the stove and flaming fuel bottle (which we most certainly felt was moments from exploding) into the stainless sink while the puddle of spilt fuel burned. My friend went from curious, dignified observer to apoplectic screamer in two milliseconds

- a great memory in the transition from city slicker to Thru-hiker that lives on to this day.

Today, especially in thru-hiking, those liquid fuel stove shenanigans have been bypassed by the canister stove and their brain-dead simplicity. Stoves like the Snow Peak Giga-Power (my favorite) with its auto ignition button or the manual (meaning you need a match) MSR Pocket Rocket are standards along the AT. At 3 ounces, on average for the stove, and a few more for the canister fuel, they offer quick, light, effortless cooking without the 2 pound load of the past. Jetboil, a full cooking system that includes the stove and pot, is also numerous along the AT. They have improved over the years, now able to simmer (instead of 100% on or a 100% off), they no longer just boil water in the blink of an eye, so you can actually cook a one pot meal. The Giga Power, Pocket Rocket, and all the alcohol and solid fuel tab stoves require getting a pot, preferably a titanium one that is just big enough to meet your food needs and still hold both your fuel canister and the stove inside for space efficiency. I also use a small stuff sack to hold my stove in before it goes inside the pot to reduce rattling. Also inside the small bag I include a one-inch square scrubbing pad and spare Bic lighter. A backup lighter is also in my "everything else" stuff sack.

Just kidding, no cast iron.

A small canister - 100 grams of isobutene/propane - can burn for about 45 minutes on high, which most hikers never do. I'd light up my stove twice each day, and with a 100 gram canister, it gave me about a week and half of hot dinners and hot chocolate afterwards. A medium canister of about 230 grams would most likely last one hiker between two to three weeks, depending on their stove use. Two hikers, with greater volumes of water, larger pot, and food would easily last a week and half with that medium size. Once again, much depends on your usage.

I constantly get asked about the different brand names of fuel, like whether you can use an MSR stove with a Jetboil canister. The manufacturers would hope you wouldn't, but yes. They are all the same, fuel-wise. The only difference is their quantity in grams and the ink printed on the outside.

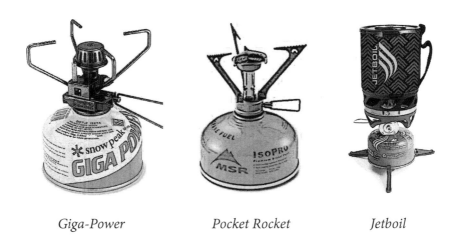

| Giga-Power | Pocket Rocket | Jetboil |

Fuel canisters are a self-sealing fuel source. So, after cooking, you unscrew the stove from the canister for easier storage. I have canisters that are ten years old and haven't lost their gas.

Canister fuel is available throughout the length of the AT, just carry a spare small or select the medium if you fret running out of canister mojo and not having a hot dinner. As pointed out in "Secret #8: Keep it easy, find it easy peasy," your stove, fuel and pot will live in your waterproof dinner food bag.

The choices are numerous if counting ounces with stoves.
Here is an assortment of alcohol and solid fuel stoves.

A long tradition in thru-hiking is the ultra-light alcohol and the solid fuel tab stoves. Made by both professional companies and a whole host of amateurs, they represent how making your own gear can be fun and simple. From two soda can bottoms shoved together or an empty cat food can with ventilation holes cut into it, each just needs some concocted potholder placed above it so the placing of the pot doesn't extinguish your flame. The creativity and variations are endless. Spending an hour watching YouTube videos can provide you with supplies and how-tos. Or just purchase one from the assorted "garage" companies. Simple. Light. Ingenious.

Denatured alcohol is the fuel of choice with these, but in a pinch, strong rubbing alcohol can suffice. You'll need to carry a small amount of denatured in some form of a bottle; I liked the 8-ounce "flask" style bottles out of REI. Because my water was filtered, I never took my dinner water to boil since I'd be unable to eat it at that temperature. I experimented and found that ¾ of an ounce of denatured alcohol would heat my one pot meals (about 12 ounces of water) just to where the bubbles formed on the bottom of the pot, rather than brought to a full roil. Certainly hot enough to hydrate the dinner and make it enjoyable to eat, but more fuel-efficient in cook time and no prolonged delay before it's in my mouth. (Yep, I'm a total efficiency nut.) Experiment to learn what works for you before starting your hike. Have a camp cook party with friends and family to show how it all will happen. Hold outdoors or keep it indoors if they have no desire to go visit nature. But keep the lights off and give everyone a headlamp for the night's festivities. You'll call it practice, they'll call it silly indoor adventure.

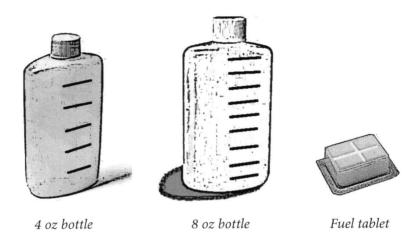

4 oz bottle   8 oz bottle   Fuel tablet

Using a Sharpie, I roughly marked the bottles in
¾ ounce increments as a helpful guide.

Solid fuel tab stoves are just as light and in some ways excel over alcohol stoves. Just have a cup-like object, put a match to a fuel brick and they burn without ash to about 1400°. They do leave a blackish residue on your stove, but that is your hiking patina that says, "this isn't my first rodeo." Sold as small, rectangular bricks (tablets, ingots, or cubes, if you prefer), each will burn about 12 minutes, so one cube per dinner and a half cube for hot chocolate after was my easy peasy system. If you light them sitting just slightly off the stove cup on a small piece of wire (YouTube it) they'll burn a bit more efficiently. You can extinguish them with a strong birthday candle blow if a shorter burn time is enough or just cut them in half. If the brick is smaller the burn time will shorten for small volume heat ups – tea, coffee or hot chocolate. Esbit may be the most notable company producing them, but there are others found on the Internet.

You can go even more primitive with your cooking if you use a wood-burning stove. Your fuel source is free and all along the trail wherever there is a forest. This type of cooking has the most connection to survival techniques and less convenient times, say during the time of Lewis and Clark. To travel the land and have a campfire taps into the romanticism of adventure, I get it, also love it. However, the AT is infamous for its wet periods. Four straight days of rain is not uncommon, so be prepared to forego a hot meal for days at such a time if you choose a wood-burning stove. All your fuel source will be wet.

I may have been one of the few that made a campfire (or attempted to make a campfire) every night on the trail. Relaxing and reflecting on the day seems easier while staring into the flickering flames. Fires at night bring a peace to everyone around camp and promote community and conversation.

Some hikers have chosen to go cold with all their dinners. They carry no stove at all. Since I strongly believe that trail happiness over the long duration of a thru-hike is tied to your food, let me just quote "Hike your own hike" and leave it at that.

 Whichever stove system or fuel source, most hikers will make one-pot meals. The noodle or rice dish you cook in your pot will also just get eaten out of it. If traveling with another person, having a bowl will then make sense.

Water. Harvesting, carrying, and drinking it.

Here's some good news for a thru-hiker: water is everywhere on the AT. The mountains provide numerous, easy sources, so you don't need to worry. This is the silver lining to all that rain that falls on your AT adventure.

Even though I'm one who counts ounces, having enough water is essential during your passage. Staying hydrated is about more than just fending off thirst. Backpacking will have you sweating profusely; replenishing those fluids will help your endurance during the day. Drinking liberal amounts will also help you avoid excruciating leg cramps from all the elevation gain and loss toil. Even cramps in fingers and hands are common when the body is low on fluids.

As the seasons advance from Spring into Summer and with it the ratcheting up of humidity and temps, hikers frequently face 90-degree temps paired with 90% humidity. Just a lovely combination for having water pour out of you. (Maybe *gush* out of you is more descriptive?) Your only choice will be to drink and drink and drink.

Almost all of us start our thru-hikes with the suburban habit of drinking water only when thirsty. This will have to change if you are to stay ahead of the hydration curve. For that reason, I'm not a fan of using water bottles. Using them means stopping, reaching, leaning your head back for a swallow or two, fumbling to get it secure again on the pack, then continuing on. All trivial actions, but they are just tedious enough to reduce your consumption. Hence, using a water reservoir with a drink tube and bite valve should be embraced. By having a drinking valve sitting on your sternum strap, you can simply stick it in your mouth while walking without missing a step or taking your eyes off the trail. These simple and effortless actions will promote a liberal intake of water.

What I recommend is to use a 3-liter reservoir, but with only 1.5 to 2 liters of water in it. When you fill your reservoir to capacity, it creates a large bulge of water that all your other gear presses against. When using 2 or less liters of water in a 3-liter reservoir it allows the water to flatten out into that extra volume, which means less bulge. This quantity should be fine in almost all distances since the locations of water sources is so accurate in the AT guidebooks. You'll even find serendipitous water trickles between those marked locations on the AT. To my memory (which is quite dubious due to inheriting it from my mother) there are only two spots where water isn't close together: South of New York's Harriman State Park, which the local hiking clubs try to rectify with water jug caches, and Pennsylvania's Lehigh Gap area around the Palmerton Super Fund pollution site. Other than those two areas, water is everywhere.

By simply carrying a guidebook and a water filter device, you can minimize water weight and yet not skimp on having it. I'm not a fan of the practice many ultra-lighters employ of only carrying minimal amounts. This always assumes that everything will go perfectly and you'll reach the next source. I'm a bit more cautious than that. Carrying a bit more water without going overboard gives you options and promotes continuous drinking.

On the extreme other side of the minimalist approach is carrying too much, as evidenced by a young hiker I met during my second thru. Not knowing about all the easy access to water or that there were guidebooks that showed you where it was, this hiker was carrying a two-and-half gallon plastic jug of water on the top of his pack, complete with a nice easy pull spout! Amazingly, it didn't stop there. In each of the young gentleman's hands was an additional one-gallon jug of water as well. He was hiking with 33-pounds of water! It was such an extreme miscalculation that I didn't say anything to the lad. There was no store to get a guidebook, and at least his load would get lighter as he went. Oh well, hike and learn. He's not the first. I've had an equally auspicious first AT experience that has helped me learn.

Yes, I have two joyful thru-hikes that were each completed in a four months and two weeks. But before I made those two savvy end-to-end journeys there was my first attempt in 2002. As crazy as it sounds, my first backpacking trip of any kind on any trail ever was a ridiculous attempt at a thru-hike of the Appalachian Trail. Unaccustomed to those things called mountains, not reading guidebooks, and not particularly fond of drinking water, I hiked 14 miles on Day 1 with less than one liter of water and ended up with excruciatingly painful leg cramps. So severe were the cramps that I limped the next few days. That first comedic thru-hiking mistake is why the other two were so smartly hiked, so it served me well.

Just in the off chance one of you is considering carrying a 54-pound backpack 14 miles with only one liter of water on Day 1 of an AT thru-hike, my advice is don't do it, don't even think it. You'd find more joy having a root-canal. Ok, moving on.

Water choreography in your hiking day.

Using a 3-liter reservoir like the Platypus Hoser (pictured below and my recommendation for its low weight and screw cap that can't come unplugged), start your hiking day with either 1.5 or 2 liters of water in it. This will keep the water weight minimal while providing enough so you can drink liberally. In addition to the Platypus Hoser, I also carried a Platypus 2-liter foldable bottle, which was kept in the same stuff sack with my water filter.

By lunchtime your reservoir should be close to empty. Take your break at a water source and fill it back up to the same level you started with. This should get you to camp later that day. Upon reaching camp and getting your sleeping bag set up on the floor of a shelter or your tent, grab that reservoir out of your backpack and your filter device. With your filter, as just mentioned, lives the Platypus 2-liter foldable bottle of the same clear material.

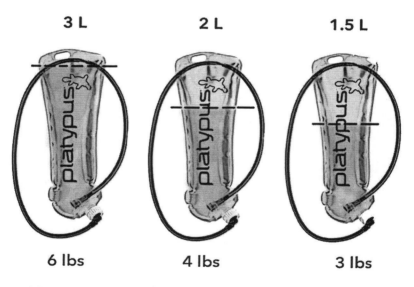

Managing water weight – having enough vs. carrying too much.

Your hiking day is over and it's time to relax and settle into the coming of dusk. Walk down to the water source, but this time fill up your 3-liter reservoir from your backpack completely. This will be your drinking water to have with dinner and through the night. Often there are nails or pegs you can hang it on next to you in the shelter. If you attach a small carabiner to its top this will make it easier. Also, fill up the 2-liter foldable bottle, this will be your dinner water, hot chocolate water, and your water for breakfast.

By morning, your 3-liter reservoir will probably be at half-full. Just drop it in your backpack after breakfast, pack up and be on your way. No need to slow your morning start by harvesting more water. You'll then repeat the lunchtime harvesting again. If there is extra filtered water in the 2-liter after breakfast, you can either pour it into your 3-liter or offer it to others around camp.

Certainly there are numerous places to put your gear in your pack, but I chose to keep my filter just underneath my top-most stuff sack (Daytime food bag) so when I open my pack I never have to dig deep when it's time to replenish my water during the hiking day.

During my hikes, the arrival in New York usually meant the hottest days with highest humidity. These were the only times where I had to pump water more than once in the hiking day. You just don't have a choice. Water is pouring out of you. Below is an illustration of what I drank on one particular day; hiking into an entrepreneurial Soda Lady added to the liquids tally that day.

From the land

ONE LITER · ONE LITER · ONE LITER · ONE LITER · ONE LITER · ONE LITER

From the Soda lady

Trail magic

Are you thirsty?
Apparently I am.

Harvesting water on the AT will come from a variety of sources. Brooks and streams are common to the mountain landscape. When faced with these sources - not knowing what may have happened upstream and is now making its way down to my harvesting position - I always used a water filter. Over the years and hikes, I've swapped out one filter for another, lightening the weight and increasing flow rate with each change. My experience was with the MSR products: first the Miniworks, then the Sweetwater, and finally the Hyperflow. I'm always looking for lightness, speed and practicality. Even though not the fastest, I like the Sweetwater for its simplistic pump action and durability. In my view, harvesting water is a time of rest and recovery. It can be a pause in the hike or a time to relax and reflect on the hiking day once you're at camp. Having an easy way to obtain it from varied sources has driven me to carrying a pump filter.

Most all filters make water clean and safe to .2 microns, thus no Giardia, and some filters go down to .1 microns! In most cases, water will be 99.99% safe. If you tend to be a worrywart, then you can use a purifier (tablets, drops or UV light) as well. I never did because it seemed a shame to ruin the pristine clean taste of cold mountain water if the chemical additives were used. That's just me and I never had an issue in 5000 miles. Instead of a filter device some will use Aqua-Mira mixed drops. These additives work well and are lightweight, but have waiting times before one can drink.

One practice I followed during my two Thru's was when water flowed right out of the side of a hill or up from the ground, then I just harvested it right into my Platypus reservoir without any form of filtration. Earth is my filter in those cases. Sometimes that will be from a PVC pipe a Trailrunner or Trail Maintenance Crew will have hammered in to ease the harvest.

These natural springs are numerous from Georgia-to-Maine. Some water sources can be quite shallow, making it more tedious to fill bottles before additives are used. Gravity fed filters are effortless, but require a deep enough pool to fill them up. Devices by Sawyer and Platypus have good flow rates at around 1.75 liters a minute without pumping, which helps when larger quantities are needed.

The Sawyer squeeze systems are ultra light and allow you to fill up their provided "dirty" water soft bottle. Once attaching their filter cartridge to their soft bottle, you squeeze the harvested "dirty" water, which pushes it through their filter device. Only just don't let your city impatience get the best of you by squeezing it too hard. Trying to increase its flow-rate by squeezing harder can break the seals of the bag/filter combo. Their .1 micron surpasses most of the competition's .2 micron filters, but .2 is all you need on the AT. Once again, the depth of the water sources makes this process of filling up squeeze bags or gravity bags a tad more tedious, but the weight savings is top notch. It is an extremely light option that doesn't ruin the flavor of the water the way chemical treatments often can. If larger quantities are needed daily, they have larger "dirty" bags that can be bought. I still like traditional filters for their broad harvesting capabilities, despite their weight and minor required labor.

Your passage of the New York miles tends to be drier than other AT sections. The local hiking clubs have left water caches to help out with our parched palettes (thank you!). My preference for filters is from a memory passing through Harriman State Park on a 90 degree day with 90% humidity. The only water source was a near invisible ten-inch hole where the water was a foot deep. The intake hose on the filter made getting it a non-issue. That hot, difficult day and that less than ideal water source has left an indelible mark that I can't shake.

There's no one way to thru-hike, so some hikers carry UV lights like a SteriPen. They make the water safe, just not clean. Bandanas can help with this, or they make a pre-filter funnel to get out the sediment, once again requiring a suitable pool of water. The funnel is easier to use when using the rigidity of a traditional water bottle. Since I've already expressed my opinion on avoiding them due to limiting your water intake, not to mention their weight and space, using a foldable bottle and a SteriPen just isn't practical.

Criteria for choosing should still be ease of use in a broad array of sources, a good flow rate speed, and a filter that filters down to .2 microns. Most filters today are field cleanable so you don't need to worry about your filter clogging while on the trail. The water on the AT is consistently in good shape and its sources numerous.

Two 1 liter bottles weigh

12.7 oz (empty)

One 2 liter foldable bottle

at 1.7 oz (empty)

Revisiting how weight is hidden in plain sight. Choosing the foldable bottle means avoiding over 1000 lbs per mile.

Secret

Things happen.

Even if you're a logistical master of planning, surprises happen in the long journey of a thru-hike. False assumptions, miscalculations, weather, broken gear, broken body parts - something may go wonky.

Even though I'm a glass-is-half-full kind of guy, I'm telling you unplanned and unwanted things will indeed happen. Being flexible will serve you well. Carrying a sense of humor in the face of all the falls and trips and bangs is strategic. You can't control the Appalachian Trail, but you can manage it. Sometimes that means stopping early in your day. Other times that will mean going longer than you planned. And some days it will mean not going at all, but staying put.

One thing I always did was have one extra dinner in my food bag for "what if's". I always had a proper form of shelter to provide options. I always carried a bit more water rather than try to perform some balancing act between running dry and the next good source. Planning only for the ideal can leave you under-equipped. I'm not saying you should hike from a glass-half-empty per-spective, but assuming all will go right is naive.

"Good judgment comes from bad experience, and a lot of that comes from bad judgment."

~ *Old Cowboy wisdom*

Let's say it's July, you've made it to the lower elevation, warmer Mid-Atlantic States, and to save weight all your insulated jackets get mailed home. Then the weather changes and instead of 80 degrees you get two weeks of 50 to 60 degree temps. Those lower temps bring along pewter skies and rain and your thinned-out, hot-weather blood makes you extra sensitive to temperature. That happened in 2006 and thru-hikers had little means to get warm, so all were getting their jackets FedExed back to the trail. Minor? Yes. Manageable? Yes. Annoying to be shivering in July? Most definitely, yes. The point is, would having one 12 oz jacket to help out if things changed be so horrific a burden of weight? Call me an ol' fuddy-duddy, but managing the texture that will find you helps you bolster your emotional strength.

As I pointed out earlier, one hiker I met came to a river ford in Virginia, a ford that didn't exist until a harsh, wet winter washed the crossing bridge away and trail crews hadn't been able to get all the resources together to construct a new one. He lost his hiking footwear while almost losing his balance during that ford. The next few days and 80- odd miles to the next resupply point (and outfitter shoe department) was hiked in his Crocs. Just nutty stuff like that can happen even with the best of precautions.

As was the case for me, when, after 4000 miles of stepping mastery, I slipped on black ice in August and broke my wrist.

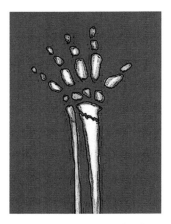

In one of my most ingenious McGyvering solutions, I used two rigid insoles (Superfeet) on each side of the wrist and then duck taped them together to immobilize the movement as a field splint. Traveling with fellow hikers Magic Shoes, Chemist, and Slim allowed for a team effort. They helped me while I helped them traverse The Whites. You never know how or when we hikers may be able to help one another.

After exiting the trail at the Mahoosuc Notch and a visit to the ER nearby, I hopped on Amtrak to heal at home. Twenty-seven days later (and a good three weeks too soon) I instructed the doctor to cut the cast off. Then, using two splints (one on top of the other), I had protection that could be temporarily removed to let an AT, rain-soaked arm dry out. On the 29th day, I was continuing northward through the infamous Mahoosuc Notch. Because I moved with purpose each day since starting in Georgia, I still had time to complete the final three weeks of Maine before the northern terminus closure. There are benefits to not being a lollygagger.

A few years back, two thru-hiking individuals lost their lives in separate events. One, upon arriving at my most favorite spot on the AT, went in for a swim in front of the shelter to relax and got leg cramps. Tragically, the young man drowned. The other hiker was discovered near the older, no longer accurate 2000 mile painted milestone in the asphalt road the AT crosses. He apparently slipped on the wet log-walk that the AT travels along in the flood prone parts of the journey, and possibly struck his head.

Today, the reason hikers cross the Kennebec River in Maine by ferry canoe - which has a white blaze painted on it – instead of fording is because a dam upstream has unannounced water releases. A hiker had the unfortunate timing to get caught in the middle of the river during one of those releases and lost their life.

Or the hiker I mentioned earlier who got a bit sloppy with staying in the moment while hiking and almost walked off a cliff while adjusting her radio. She got lucky. Things happen during an Appalachian Trail thru-hike. But those things are miniscule to how many injure themselves while taking selfies or putting their phone as priority one and driving the car as priority two. Remain flexible and be willing to zag, it can keep you moving forward. The trail is splendidly difficult and some injuries are only delays, not denials.

Birds do it. Bees do it.

So why should hikers be any different? Since we've all gotten to know each other over the course of this book (sort of), let's get it out in the open. Let's talk SEX – trail sex to be specific.

Let's talk trail romance, infatuation, and displays of such - not necessarily in that order. As the saying goes, "It finds you when you aren't looking."

When you look at the social dynamic of a bunch of hikers all gathering nightly at the same locations to share joys, miseries, and common aspirations, bonds between hikers will happen. For those of you staying put, guarding the home front, while your significant goes walkabout, there is good news. Most of these new friendships will be strictly platonic. However, a few will become deeper. Since no one has their pose clothes on (little black dress, heels, blazer, and bling) to elevate their confidence, we reveal to others what is at our core. Our insecurities (and some dirt) follow us into camp looking for fellowship with a, "Hey, everybody." The sharing of this common purpose to achieve a thru-hike may be the ideal icebreaker.

Echoing our childhood practice of passing notes in class, the shelter registers allow flirtation to bloom up and down the AT. Only here in the timeframe of a thru-hike, a note to others in the shelter registers can be foreplay. Does getting lucky become less about reaching Mt. Katahdin and more about "getting lucky"?

Can you imagine meeting some hotty after several days of smelly sweating, no shower or fresh laundry, where your cologne is Thru-Hike Stench No.5, and try to make a good impression? Sort of brings new meaning to eau de toilette. Or scenarios where you've just met and you're seen grabbing your TP and marching off into the woods? Not exactly sugar and spice and everything nice, huh? I'm guessing if two can leap beyond such a colorful beginning and still find attraction, there may indeed be some promise.

Could a one-month anniversary together be the gift of a Snickers bar of love rather than a bouquet of roses? How thoughtful to pass over 250 calories that they didn't have to carry – now *that's* trail magic.

Without doors anywhere to open, could a man prove his infatuation by sweeping a shelter floor space for his new companion's mummy? Or as she hikes out in the morning, she presents him with that seductive look back over her shoulder that says, "Hike with me." And how wonderful that there's no awkward goodnight kiss or come-up-for-a-nightcap moment since you both know you're going to sleep together – even if it really is sleep. And let's not forget the romance hurdle that you'll also be sleeping with Bob, Carol, Ted, and Alice in the same shelter. (Only they'll be known as Bear Bait, Pokey, No Doubt, and Fordo.)

A thru-hike strips away all the posturing and games and lets two people really see who they are. The hardships reveal frailties and strengths - qualities easily hidden in the distractions of the normal dating world. Do the female thru-hikers become more self-conscious about unshaven legs? Can smitten men stop fretting over when to phone or what to say if they have to leave a message?

As the attraction blooms, so does the placement of your mummies. Where you once looked for a single slot on the shelter floor, you now look for two. And how wonderful it must be to share a pot of Ramen together where the grandest of gestures to a fellow thru-hiker is, "Oh, please, you take the last bite." Yes, we're talking L - O - V - E.

It must be an incredible surprise to walk off into the wilderness expecting isolation and oneness with nature and finding romance, possibly even your soul mate. You expected to find birds and bees, but not the birds-and-the-bees. Although the cuddling-giggle fests over in the corner of the shelter become a tad annoying come dark when most just want to sleep and dream of food

- glorious food. I like that people find each other on the trail and fall in love.

Amorous hikers do face certain wilderness challenges of, hmm...let's say, having more intimate knowledge of their new sidekick (pun not intended, but welcomed). If they start as a solo hiker, that could mean each, most likely, has a 1-person tent - drats! Forget about it if they started with a hammock, they'd end up falling on their head with a concussion rather than satisfaction. This all begs the question that if one shows up to hike solo but has a two-person tent, is that not being presumptuous on their part (or just hopeful)? Of course, it's safe to say that town stops, which are usually about all things food and resupply, certainly do take on a whole new significance.

During my two thru-hikes I got great adventure and a wonderful first book of my journey. It also led to a change in my priorities and a new life direction - pretty much a "9" on a scale of ten. But that pales to those lucky, wonderful few who find love. When my hike was over I returned home with fabulous memories. Some of you, however, will return home with something a tad more significant: a spouse.

The Greatest Mountain.

Months ago, hikers pointed themselves toward the horizon. With apprehension and exuberance a step was taken. What lay in front of them was completely unknown. Finding the rhythm of traillife they moved farther forward. As the land changed from spring to summer to fall, they followed suit, evolving from suburbanites to adventurers. For the northbounders, they emerge from the Hundred Mile Wilderness to a logging road. It is there at Abol Bridge that the postcard majesty of Mt. Katahdin greets them.

On a clear day, the eye candy moment is a thing to behold. The awe and grandeur will imprint its indelible mark. Standing here means months of grit and perseverance of thru-hiking will soon earn them a new title, a christening: Thru-hiker. The purity, the uncluttered ecstasy of viewing what the Penobscot Indians called The Greatest Mountain will fill these bold few with childlike glee. Still a dozen miles from its shadow, hikers are now living in its presence. No longer a word, no longer a mysterious place in the ether of the trail. As many reflect on this moment, an enormous bird may take flight off a pine, its unmistakable white head and tail contrasted against the dark evergreen. Another great trail moment to join the countless others.

After some treats at the Abol Bridge Camp Store, they float along the rest of the day through the spruce, hemlock and fir to the final staging area at Katahdin Stream Campground for one final sunset, one final campfire and one final night under The Milky Way.

When a Park Ranger returns to the visitor center after morning rounds, hikers register their intentions to summit The Greatest Mountain and declare if they're a Northbounder, Southbounder or Flip-flopper. They learn what hiker number they are to reach this destination. When I had placed my foot by that first white blaze on Springer Mountain in Georgia, an Appalachian Trail Conservency ambassador informed me that I was number 1580-something. When my legs walked me up the steps at the ATC headquarters in Harpers Ferry a thousand miles later, I was 534. A Polaroid was taken and my trailname and arrival number were Sharpied on and slid in a notebook. Now, an almost incomprehensible passage of time later, I was 286.

To arrive here most assuredly means one found the joy of the journey. Although rain found a full one-third of my days that first thru-hike, I discovered strategies that prevented my spirit from being dampened, strategies that would provide easier passage on my second journey. Although a broken wrist a day after crossing into Maine would find me on my second thru-hike, it was just another obstacle to step over.

The rest of the day is for appreciation of this location, one so impossibly far away from where that small stone was selected with care (not too big, not to small) and pocketed - a tradition that has lived on through the decades. Although each hiker got here for different reasons, all decided that life could no longer be postponed. That words like "someday" needed to be vanquished. Hikers know there's still more to be done though - more mountain to maneuver. If it is still hard to believe you're here, a stroll over to the village green lets you gaze upward. There, thousands of feet above, it sits inviting you to visit. The finish line.

The Rangers post tomorrow's hiking forecast as one of four classifications. Class One means the trail is open and conditions are favorable; Class Two means the trail is open but not recommended, conditions favorable but could be changing; Class Three means some trails are open but not recommended due to conditions; Class Four means mandatory closure of all Mt. Katahdin trails.

Blessed with a Class One day for my first completion and a Class Two my second due to black ice that would melt, I was able to move forward with both planned summits without consequence. It seemed fitting my last climb for thru-hike #2 had some black ice, as my wrist was just seven weeks healed since my previous run-in with the stuff.

I would like to say that hikers will sleep soundly knowing that 99% of the journey is behind them, knowing that they've polished their hiking skills in the sharp granite edges and weather theatrics, and yet 5.2 miles of up still gives them pause. Even with sixteen Mt. Everest's under their tread, knowing they've been transformed into mountain athletes, respect for the biggest ascent of the journey is willingly given. Hikers know better than to get cocky, know that there are no guarantees. The Appalachian Trail never relaxes - it saves its biggest climb for the crescendo of this hiking symphony. And oh what a high note it is.

Over these past months, hikers have honed their mastery of the land. They now carry confidence in their backpacks. Their legs are coiled and the lungs and pulse are at lifetime slowness due to their elevated fitness. Their rediscovered patience battles their exuberance that there is only one more day of up left, while their trail savvy softly whispers, "Things can still happen." That Georgia morning back in March or April will share a cold chill with tomorrow's start here in Maine. Hopefully skies will be clear with blue; a hint of frost will likely be in the air. Red, yellow and orange leaves say it is getting late, not many days left in the season. Only one more will be all that's needed.

Come morning, hikers make their way to the trailhead where a sign-in board acts as starting line. Hikers mark the time they start. Upon their return, a sign-out lets the Park Rangers know whether they have a situation on their hands. Since all who hike come to the AT with different abilities, the time it takes to reach the summit varies. Many who come off a sofa for a day-hike up Mt. Katahdin may see timeframes of six or more hours, sometimes smartly turning back to avoid darkness issues. Getting there as a thru-hiker though, you are now a super-you, now a climbing machine; four hours is totally doable. On both of my ascents, once "Postcard" was scribbled on the clipboard, I never stopped, never even remotely considered needing a rest. The achievement within my grasp powering me ever higher, my patience learned over 2000 miles evaporated.

The climb starts with the typical upward ramp of trail and rocks with big step-ups that zig and zag, a ruggedness one has gotten familiar with in Maine. One settles into a rhythm that will continue up this largest climb of the entire thru-hike. After an hour plus of forest ascent, hikers reach a befuddling mass of giant boulders that brings them above treeline. Figuring the route isn't as clear - choices to go left or right can be made. It is here where hiking poles become less useful since grabbing rock edges and rebar handles help one to move higher. A pause to take in the grandeur to your backside provides countless photo memories. If a fear of heights is your undoing, don't turn around. Best to keep facing the mountain and climb rather than see where you actually are. (You'll get to bask in this beauty, or panic, as the case may be, on the way down.) The next time you'll pass through here a euphoric fog and a new title will be traveling with you: AT Thru-Hiker.

The Gateway

Shielded from directional winds, hikers emerge to the unnerving Gateway where exposure to the elements is at its highest. The first time I climbed Mt Katahdin, having never seen this mountain, knowing nothing about the climb, the Gateway presented me with a steep spine, a knife-edge similar to where two sides of a pyramid meet. The Gateway ascent disappeared into a shroud of wind-whipped clouds and fog ribbons racing over its unwelcoming edge. It was a fear-inducing, anxiety-gulp moment for even my Super Postcard version of myself. No longer able to see the climb, the disappearing ragged "trail" stopped me in my tracks. Now with thousands of miles of hiking experience, I refocused my eyes downward to the rock, downward to the white blazes and stopped looking up to the unknown. Getting myself realigned with my Stay-In-The-Moment strategy, the journey continued upward. It was scary, the unknown always is. Not once on that first climb through The Gateway did I ever look up; it was that intense for me. The narrow spine of the Gateway drops off significantly on both sides, giving others even braver than me hesitation. I know one hiker who started in Georgia, but was unable to make it through this area and failed to complete.

As for the stepping texture itself, imagine walking on the tops of your fingers. The rocks are not flat and wide, they are rounded pedestals with gaps requiring all your stepping prowess, focus and confidence. Usually a dramatic section like the Gateway ends at the summit in our storybook minds, but for Mt. Katahdin it is different. At the top of the Gateway, Katahdin rewards all those who make its passage with a more gentile ramp of easier walking called The Tablelands. It is here on a clear day that a small bump on the summit a mile away can just be made out – a bump made of wood boards and legs anchored in the granite chunks. It won't be long now; you are closing in on Baxter Peak, the northern terminus of the Appalachian Trail. You check your pocket, good, your small Springer Mountain stone is still with you.

Here your pace quickens. By now hikers are not only above treeline, they're above the clouds. Although the trails difficulty subsides, one can never relax. Faster and faster hikers get pulled to that famous Katahdin sign that sits 5270 feet above sea level - not the AT's highest point, but its most dramatic. Trying to stay in the moment with your footing, ever resisting the urge to keep looking up at the distant bump because you know events can still happen. Falling can still happen. Injury can still happen. You hike and look and hike and look; it's nearly impossible not to keep glancing up, watching the summit inch ever closer. If the wind is present on your summit day, the higher you progress, the higher its speed. You stay focused, at a half-mile, the sign and its "A" frame shape emerge. One hundred feet, Fifty, Twenty, Ten, and then you touch it, hug and embrace this landmark that has lived timelessly in photos. Resting your face upon its weather-beaten surface, a flood of warmth washes over you. Some will tear up, others will go quiet, but most all will be engulfed in a euphoric haze.

Photos will be taken, corks popped and small stones deposited on the Baxter Peak cairn where they may whisper, "There, it's complete." Some who make it may reflect on moments a thousand miles earlier where a critical decision during a low moment was made to continue. Others overcame life itself, deciding that this journey was more important than anything else they could possibly do. The lucky ones are those who with absolute clarity never, ever, considered the possibility of stopping. For them there was no happier place or activity; their thru-hike was a mission of joy.

Some will be glad it's over. Others like myself will revel in the moment, but not truly needing it to end. It's fabulous to cross a finish line, but who really wants an activity that makes one happy to stop? Both climbs up Mt. Katahdin took me 2 hours 45 minutes, although it felt like only 45 – the climber's trance I suppose?

No longer warmed by forward motion, lingering at this site above the clouds tends to be cold when most Thru-hikers arrive. I remember staring at the Katahdin sign for long periods with every stitch of clothing on, hypnotized by all it meant. Trying to comprehend the time and distance that had elapsed – and failing to do so. I've had numerous honors bestowed on me for my efforts though life. Reaching this monument to adventure is the one I bestowed onto myself.

One thing is clear, a Thru-hiker has achieved one of the greatest individual adventures one can achieve. This journey of discovery may reorder your priorities, even change your life's direction. But first, there's still one small matter that needs to be addressed. Everyone still has 5.2 miles of descent to hike before dark - a piece of cake for a Thru-hiker.

Your exit.

What happens next in a completed thru-hike is a bit odd. Twenty miles away is Millinocket, Maine, the exit town that will start your re-entry back to the normal world. Only you no longer have to walk to it, you can now get in a car and ride.

At the Appalachian Trail Cafe & Lodge, one can soften their transition back to metropolis by surrounding oneself with walls and rooms covered in thru-hiking illustrations, illustrations capturing the texture one just lived the past many months. Some will trigger a giggle, some a smile and some a "Glad I don't have to do that again!" moment. All were drawn during my two thru-hikes, postcards from Postcard.

Every so often one of you steals an image that touches a nerve and then they call me for a replacement. So don't steal the art; you're still an ambassador for the trail.

You'll submit your completion achievment to the ATC offices in Harpers Ferry. A Certificate of Congratulations with your name on it (real name, that is) will arrive shortly thereafter, along with a small swatch of fabric with thread embroidery that signifies that you per-servered, rose above all nature of adversities. It says you no longer let life be postponed, you stepped out to live boldly and to not only dream of greener grass over the horizon, you wiggled your toes in it. With honor, integrity and I suppose a bit of hare-brained nuttiness, you completed the entirety of The Appalachian Trail. Although your distance travelled was farther, its phrasing is a nod to tradition, to history and its original length. Display it proudly - it is significant. Well done, you are a "2000-Miler". A Thru-hiker. Whatever your path moving forward, you'll find you may do so standing a bit taller.

Post-hike adjustments.

After all the roots and rocks, after the ups and downs and tilted terrain, newly christened Thru-hikers get to face a new challenge: post-hike withdrawal.

That time when all we've known and embraced eagerly is taken away – despite its difficulty, splendidly trying at times, the absence of the journey's stimuli leaves a void and that hits each of us differently. Post-hike adjustments are common – some call it Re-entry, others label it as returning to the normal world. Whatever the description, we all receive a re- introduction in the days and weeks (and next seasons) after the trail's final terminus.

For me, adjusting to indoor life with its indoor air influenced by fabrics, carpet, linens, and last night's dinner aroma instead of evergreens, moss, and flowers was wholly unsatisfying. Can you remember that toasty scent given off by beds of pine needles roasting in the midday sun? Anyone following my shenanigans along the AT over the years knows my love of what I've coined Christmasland – the summit balsam fir and spruce trees and their holiday aroma. Loooove it. I missed living in that epic fresh air – sleeping in it, taking it in by the lungful and swallowing it like double fudge chocolate cake. This addiction has resulted in patio doors left ajar and bedroom windows forever cracked regardless of the weather. Twice now my fresh air dependence has forced me to pull out my wallet and park a convertible in the driveway. Rolling down windows and opening a sunroof is helpful, but an unobstructed, limitless roof of blue sky and endless headroom has no comparison. Some of you may be stronger than I to fight off these feelings. As for me, though, I'm a weakling to the Siren song of a fresh breeze resulting from my thru-hikes.

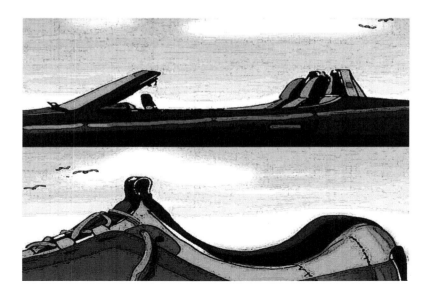

A thru-hike messes me up. It shows me what's possible through the gifts that only nature can deliver and then never lets me forget its kiss. Nature plays hard-to-forget. Every so often, here at home, I'll be in the backyard and a breeze with its invisible, subtle scent will appear for the briefest of moments and I'll think, "The Trail." They say that smell triggers our strongest memories, so it shouldn't come as a surprise, should it? Those magic moments of AT air that wafts its way to my backyard touches my heart – what an incredible longing for more of a good thing. Back in the normal world, the cockpit of my convertible serves as a tonic – my self-prescribed fresh air therapy. Until my shoes can take over the responsibilities again, my roofless wonder helps me tolerate all things not trail.

This fresh air withdrawal always grows worse around springtime of each new year when it hops on the back of Springer Mountain fever. If you don't get handcuffed to the bedpost, your fate will likely have you answering to a trailname for another five months. That's how I ended up thru-hiking a second time. Most of us - me for one - couldn't imagine doing more than one thru-hike before our first. (And I have a pretty fair talent for imagining things.)

Immediately after my thru-hikes, it was challenging to remember to put on different clothes each day. Or wear deodorant. Or that I no longer needed to count squares of toilet paper. Or to police myself from consuming entire pies. Once you discover the true splendor of a life simply lived, some old habits have to be relearned. Silly, trivial things still persist, such as given a choice between a fork or a single large spoon, I still choose the spoon. Instead of killing bugs that make it into the house, they're now caught and released to the out-doors...I learned the suburban world is not mine alone, but rather I share it with them just as I did on the trail.

Our toes certainly had faced more than their share of toebox slams – sixteen Mr. Everest's will do that – many times they'll have some numbness afterwards (actually, a lot of numbness). I learned from others that full feeling would return after 3 months, and sure enough, my big toe's full sensation returned in December after my September summits.

I look up more now too, to the clouds, at the gliding wings above me to judge if it's a raptor or scavenger. When you share the wild world on a primitive level, appreciation for your companions grows stronger. Priorities of the past may (will) reorder themselves. Once driven by cityness go-go, I had driven faster than the speed limit everywhere for decades and decades. No longer do I wish to do that. Discovering world-class patience, no longer feeling I'm behind, I gladly stick to the right "slow" lane and let others merge in front of me, not remotely feeling I'm less of a person for letting it happen.

Fresh air, large spoons, and driving the speed limit are my top three, but there is a fourth. Having managed Mother Nature and her wrath like lightning storms on summits, hurricane-swollen fords, and thousands and thousands of miles in the wilderness, I have less tolerance for those individuals who turn molehills into mountains with their unbalanced drama fits. Standing tall when the winds of life start to blow is and always will be a measure of one's character. These people get little of my time – an area I'm trying to improve on.

Shortly after my second thru-hike, both my father and sister were diagnosed with Stage 4 cancers. The emotional strength and patience learned over the course of 4000 miles enabled me to pay tribute on behalf of the family at both of their funerals. The humility, relearned in the face of all those very democratic mountains where we're all created equal, has also brought more balance to this once over-achieving advertising executive. Relaxing of one's ego doesn't mean you become a sloth. If the thru-hike reinforces anything, it is you don't make progress unless you move with purpose.

Anyway, those are my post-hike shifts. Maybe yours will be a desire to pee in your backyard? Or anywhere, anytime when the urge hits you? I knew a woman who after her hike couldn't stop sleeping in her hammock outside, she loved it so much – played hell with her sex life, though.

Do anything for month after month, especially when it makes you sing spontaneously, and there's going to be some adjustment.

#1

#2

Your turn. Katahdin is waiting.

"May your dry sock days be more numerous than the wet ones and may your smiles always outnumber your miles."

~ M.E. "Postcard" Hughes

About Postcard.

Years ago, I was described as being equal parts George Patton and Walt Disney. Nothing's changed.

I've been to all 50 United States, even walked through 14 of them.

I believe individuals can make a difference.

After 9/11, three words appeared within me: "Never postpone life". That's why I thru-hiked the AT before retirement.

One can never smile too much, that's why I thru-hiked the AT a second time.

I respect people who stand tall when the winds start to blow. Both my sister and father stood the tallest during their losing battles with cancer.

As a result, I struggle to respect those who turn molehills into mountains.

I walk with purpose, attack projects and miles, and am made joyful in doing so.

I've never chased money, but rather chased the things that I was passionate about, which made me money.

I'm a glass-is-half-full person.

I like being courteous, kind and helpful. You'll often hear me greet my friends with a "Hello Gorgeous" or a "Hello Handsome" to make them feel great.

When interested in a subject or endeavor, I tend to excel at it.

During my top business years, I didn't know how to nurture others. It's a regret that I now try to rectify.

We should look to fix problems rather than fix blame.

I believe profanity is the product of a lazy mind.

Most problems are simply decisions we haven't made.

I believe age is a mindset. If you think you're old, you are. If you're old, but have a youthful mindset, you're youthful.

Where I shop for groceries, there's a small hill down to the parking lot. I still hop on the cart and ride it with glee.

I like Abe Lincoln's quote: "Folks are usually about as happy as they make their minds up to be." This has a correlation with succeeding at a thru-hike.

Some call me Mark. Others call me Uncle Mark. When they can start talking, some will call me Great Uncle Mark. And still others call me Postcard.

My middle name is Errol, after my grandfather's first name, my father's middle name, and the Hollywood swashbuckler Errol Flynn – which is totally appropriate.

I'm a dog, cat, owl, loon, moose, koi, frog, turtle, woodpecker, dove, hawk, and eagle person.

I'd rather pick up a discovered feather or rock as a souvenir than any knickknack found in a gift shop.

Conifers are my favorite trees, but I have a deep appreciation for Japanese maples.

The wood smoke smell of a campfire beats out the most intoxicating perfume in my book. (Of course, there are exceptions.)

Having flown over a million miles, today I'd rather take a train or drive.

The longest road trip I've taken was 16,000 miles to visit our National Parks. Everyone should visit them, only I'm glad they don't so the Parks stay quieter.

The morning I drove into Manhattan to start a career in advertising was the 16th of September. Sixteen years later, I drove out on the 16th of September. Didn't see a single shooting star in all that time. Sixteen days later I saw one.

I once witnessed the Aurora Borealis from 40,000 feet for four hours. I was glued to the airplane window during a return flight from Japan.

I've had my life threatened three times – all on the same trip. The circumstances involved a rather large African bull elephant, a white rhinoceros, and a male lion.

I grew up in a family where both parents were the breadwinners. Dad did the cooking.

I'm at my happiest when I'm creating.

After carrying a backpack over 5000 miles, I've discovered that simplicity is one of life's truly great pleasures.

Four of my top memories of achievement are walking across the stage in college, sharing top honors and hearing those I competed against cheer and applaud. Walking across the stage at Lincoln Center in New York in front of 2000 applauding professionals, accepting the top honor for an advertisement I created. Standing in front of 200 cheering equals as they honored me with REI's highest award: The Anderson Award. And embracing a weather-beaten sign buried in granite, above the clouds atop The Greatest Mountain, an honor I bestowed upon myself to absolute silence.

I believe that a thru-hike is one of the greatest gifts you can give to yourself.

And I'm still puzzled why so many try to park as close as they can to the front door of their health clubs.